MW00475402

MYSTICAL INTERLUDES

An Ordinary Person's Extraordinary Experiences

MYSTICAL INTERLUDES

An Ordinary Person's Extraordinary Experiences

A Memoir

Emily Rodavich

© 2016 by Emily Rodavich.

All rights reserved. No part of this book may be reproduced by any mechanical, photographic, or electronic process, or in the form of a phonographic recording; nor may it be stored in any retrieval system, transmitted, or otherwise copied for private or public use—other than for "fair use" as brief quotations embodied in articles and reviews—without prior written permission from the publisher. Email: Permissions@CitrinePublishing.com.

Limit of Liability/Disclaimer of Warranty: While the publisher and author have used their best efforts in preparing this book, they make no representations or warranties with respect to the accuracy or completeness of the contents of this book and specifically disclaim any implied warranties of merchantability or fitness for a particular purpose. The author of this book does not dispense medical advice or prescribe the use of any technique as a form of treatment for physical, emotional, or medical problems without the advice of a physician. The intent of the author is only to offer information of a general nature to help you in your quest for well-being. In the event you use any of the information in the book for yourself, which is your constitutional right, the author and publisher assume no responsibility for your actions.

Editing and interior design: Penelope Love · *Cover design:* Rolf Busch

Library of Congress Cataloging-in-Publication Data

Rodavich, Emily.
Mystical Interludes: An Ordinary Person's Extraordinary Experiences.

p. cm.
Paperback ISBN: 978-0-9975470-0-9
Digital ISBN: 978-0-9975470-1-6
Library of Congress Control Number: 2016942765
10 9 8 7 6 5 4 3 2 1
1st Edition, July 2016

CITRINE PUBLISHING

Boca Raton, Florida, U.S.A.
561.299.1150
Publisher@CitrinePublishing.com
www.CitrinePublishing.com

To those who inspired me,

Veronica, my teacher, Jim, my love

and

To those for whom this book was written,

Marion Geruschat

Stephen Geruschat

Cara Geruschat Cullen

and progeny

ACKNOWLEDGMENTS

Jim Flenniken, my best friend and partner in everything, you started me on my journey to writing this book when you said to me, "Get started today!" Jim, you've been with me every step of the way, picking me up when I was down and cheering me on to the finish. Your devoted attention to my every technical need and your tireless support as reader, advisor, researcher, and housemate have been superlative. Know that I couldn't have accomplished this book without you, my love.

Nancy Aloi Rose, my friend and confidante, you were the first person outside of Jim to read my rudimentary story draft. Nancy, even though you are one of the busiest people I know, you are always there for me. Your love and encouragement spurred me on.

Doug Weed, it was my good fortune to meet you at the Pittsburgh South Writers Group. After reading your unpublished poetry, I knew I had met a man of letters. It didn't take long for me to realize that you have one of the sharpest minds I've ever encountered! You have been more than generous in all you've given in editing time and guidance. I am ever grateful to you, dear friend, for helping me find my voice and encouraging me to see myself as a writer.

Marion Geruschat, my daughter, you read several drafts via email also during my last visit to you in Hawaii. Marion, your suggestions, love, and support have carried me. Your enthusiastic faith in me works like a drug to make me more than I am.

Lynn Krug, my friend, you studied an early draft from beginning to end. Lynn, you invested yourself in carefully editing punctuation, inconsistencies, and missing details. Thank you again for helping me forward on this journey.

Mark Fazzolari, your friendship has enriched my spirituality and served as an inspiration for writing this memoir. Through you, Mark, I met my outstanding editor and publisher, Penelope Love. Your introduction to Penelope fulfilled my wish to find the right person who would guide me to the success of publishing my book.

Penelope: thank you, thank you, not only for your professional expertise, but also for your joyful spirit and positive attitude every step of the way. You have made this first-time venture into publishing fun for me!

Life can only be understood backwards;

but it must be lived forwards.

Søren Kierkegaard

TABLE OF CONTENTS

INTRODUCTION

Has anything like this happened to you?

- After praying to God, you wait for an answer. Then it comes unexpectedly into your mind. It is unexpected because it is not the answer you would have chosen for yourself. Later you realize it was the *perfect* answer.

- The memory of a recently deceased loved one fills your thoughts. The emotional bond you shared resonates in your heart. At that moment you hear a sound or a song that *informs* you that your loved one is letting you know he/she is there.

- By happenstance you arrive somewhere just in time to save a person from harm or death. Later you feel you were guided to the location.

- Without thinking you write out factual information you had no way of knowing beforehand.

- You have an unexpected vision of a past life.

- You have a life-changing near-death experience.

If you have experienced any of those extraordinary events you might be reluctant to talk about them with friends or family, as I was.

After living through those phenomena and more, I was left with a burning desire to share them with someone who'd had similar experiences or had some insight into such things. But most of my friends, to my knowledge, had not met with such mystical occurrences. I was afraid they'd think I was crazy or weird if I tried to describe my experiences to them. Until now I've been selective in deciding with whom I could share my secrets. That has changed.

To be clear, I am not a psychic. Nor am I a psychic wannabe.

What I am is an ordinary person who has stumbled into the supernatural zone at different times and in different ways. At ages seven and eight, I personally experienced God in my life when I received answers to sincere and desperate prayers. That profound awakening opened for me a door to spirituality.

Outside of praying I've never intentionally invoked any of my transcendent encounters, nor have I tried. Each was unplanned and unexpected. Most of them took me by complete surprise, seeming to pop into my life without warning. Sometimes they temporarily jumbled my reality, leaving me with more questions than answers.

Now in my later years I'm content and secure in my skin. I've come to realize that those powerful experiences have been extraordinary gifts that should be shared rather than closeted.

It's my hunch that the world is full of ordinary people like myself who have been surprised by similar incidents. It's time we come forward and share them with each other and the world around us. I have come to believe that our Supreme Being—God, Father, Creator, Higher Power, Being or Universe—whichever name you choose from a seemingly endless list—communicates with each of us in ways suited to our readiness.

Far be it from me to define the meaning of *readiness* for

either myself or anybody else. To clarify my meaning, I think it has something to do with an individual's perception of God and also one's threshold of fear. As I said earlier, most of my experiences left me with more questions than answers, often leaving me in a state of initial confusion.

For this book I have chosen ten mystical interludes to describe in detail, even though I have experienced more than these over the years. My purpose in selecting these ten is to reveal the various *kinds* of phenomena that have punctuated my life.

They include, among others, "hearing" answers to prayers, visiting myself in a past life, and dreaming a winning number. My hope is that by chronicling these mysterious incidents, I am giving affirmation to people, young and old, who have experienced, or are experiencing similar events.

Regardless of who you are, may the narratives within these pages broaden your awareness and inspire you to continue exploring the boundless universe of your life.

YESTERDAY

VERONICA'S SECRETS

My mother Veronica was clairvoyant. I know this because I personally witnessed three of her episodes. These happenings convinced me that extrasensory perception is real.

The first event occurred in 1956 when I was a teenager. It's the only one she told me about before it happened. At the time I was unaware of the influence it would have on my life.

Mom and I were at the kitchen sink doing dinner dishes. She washed and I dried. Her busy hands in the soapy dishwater suddenly stopped moving and she stood gazing out the window. I wondered what was wrong. *Was she all right? Was she staring at something outside the window?*

She turned and looked at me solemnly. "I think Grandpap Eli is going to die soon."

"What?" Her words surprised me. "What makes you think that?" My dad's father had been briefly hospitalized a year earlier for a mild heart condition. Since that time, his prescribed medication seemingly kept him well.

She returned her gaze to the window. I wondered what was going on in her head.

"Has Grandpap been sick?" I asked.

"Not that I know of," she answered, "but I had a vivid dream last night of going to their house after his funeral. Cars pulled up in front. I saw your dad near tears helping Grandma out of the car. She was crying into a large white handkerchief. As I climbed the steps to the front porch, I felt a runner slide up the stocking at the back of my right leg."

"Oh. It was just a dream, then," I drawled. At least it explained her brief space-out. I added, "Grandpap's been looking pretty good to me. He works in his garden all the time. He gave us vegetables the last time we visited. Remember? He's fine."

Mom's dream paled in significance to my personal interests. My thoughts at the time were consumed by my own circumstances. I was still reeling from an almost fatal illness a few months earlier that had led to a near-death experience. I had also just started a new job. If that weren't enough, my teenage mind was beset with thoughts of a special guy.

A week or two later, my granddad walked out his back door at sunrise to survey his garden in the light of the morning sky, as was his habit. When he didn't return to the kitchen as usual, Grandma went looking for him. She was stunned and broken hearted to find him lying in his garden where he took his last breath at age seventy-four, the morning of October 13, 1956.

The news of my grandfather's sudden death shocked our family. Everybody wanted to know why and how he died. Grandma refused an autopsy, saying, "He's gone. Nothing can bring him back. What does it matter how he died?" The coroner's report gave his cause of death as heart failure.

The funeral was held several days later. I don't remember linking Mom's dream to Grandpap's death, but something happened that day that brought it all back.

After the burial service, family cars, one by one, parked in the broad grassy area outside the gate to my grandparents' home. Neighbors waited inside to serve a traditional meal to the family of mourners.

As I followed Mom up the steps to the front porch, I watched a runner slide up the nylon stocking of her right leg. Her "dream" popped into my head like a shot. Tapping her on the shoulder, I gasped, "Mom! You got a runner! It's just like you..."

Before I could finish she took my hand and squeezed, "I know, I know," she said, holding her finger to her lips. "Let's not talk about it."

We didn't talk about it again that day but I brought it up at home a few days later. "Your dream came true, Mom, down to the runner in your stocking. That's pretty amazing!" I exclaimed. "How do you think that happened?"

"Oh, I don't know," she said dismissively as though we were wondering about a stain on the tablecloth. "Everybody dreams," she added casually.

"Yes, but not everybody dreams about things that actually happen!" I answered emphatically.

"I don't have an answer," she said calmly, "so I don't dwell on it. You shouldn't either. It's best just to let it go."

"But, Mom, don't you realize how amazing your dream was? I told Joanne and Lois about it and they said you're psychic!"

Her voice was sharp. "Emily Ann, I don't want you telling another soul about that dream! I am *not* psychic! And I don't want anybody to describe me that way! Do you understand me?"

"Not really," I said, confused by her sudden vehemence.

"I'm asking you to respect my feelings. Please promise me you won't tell anybody else about that dream—especially not your father or his family." She was scowling at me. I knew her relationship with my dad's family was often shaky, for soon after my parents were married, one of Dad's sisters planted a rumor that Mom had seduced Dad into marrying her. Even though almost two decades had elapsed since then, a thin wire of tension ran between Mom and some members of the Rodavich family—at least in Mom's perception.

Her intensity got through to me. I felt as though I'd betrayed her in some way by telling my friends. "OK, Mom, I won't talk about it again," I said apologetically.

"Thanks, honey," she said, stepping forward to give me a hug. "It's important to me."

I kissed her on the cheek and we went our separate ways in the house. I was curious about why she was so secretive about her amazing dream.

Then there was the question of how it happened. What caused her to have that dream? Although I had no answers, I knew one thing for sure: she had been able to see the future.

There was nothing personally strange about my mother; however, she did have an unconventional childhood. If she was unusual, it was because of the fearless and determined way she prevailed through her life's challenges.

Veronica, eventually a sibling to four sisters and three brothers, was raised as an only child from birth by her immigrant maternal grandparents. They doted on her and, speaking little English themselves, taught her to speak their Czechoslovakian language.

When Veronica turned eight, her beloved grandmother died. Bereaved, she was forced to rejoin her parents and four siblings, of whom she was second in age. Although she was an outsider, Veronica was expected to pitch in with chores and childcare for the younger ones, including three babies born later.

Such upheaval early in life—the loss of her surrogate mom who was replaced by an almost strange new mother—and her need to adapt from being an only child to being one of five, might have weirded out most kids. Young Veronica persevered.

Then the Great Depression hit, threatening the very survival of unemployed coal miners and their families, especially large families. At age thirteen, after having completed eight grades of Catholic school under the scrutiny of stern nuns who cracked students on their knuckles with the edges of wooden rulers, Veronica was eager to leave school and help support her family.

Relatives living in New York City sent word to the small coalmining town in Pennsylvania informing Mom's family that jobs for housekeepers and nannies were plentiful in certain parts of the city. Heeding their advice, Veronica, barely fourteen, and her sister Margaret, seventeen, donned the best of their few dresses and rode several buses many long hours until they were finally delivered into the strange, huge metropolis. Shortly after they arrived, both teenage girls had the good fortune of being hired by wealthy families with children.

Mom spoke affectionately of the Shapiro family who employed her. Nevertheless, after fifteen months of being homesick, she returned to her Pennsylvania home and took a job at the local bakery.

Weeks later she met a handsome young coal miner, Steve Rodavich, and fell in love. They were married within six months.

I've often wondered when my mother discovered her clairvoyance. I've also wondered how often she experienced it throughout her years, and to what extent. Answers to these questions remain unknown to me because of her reluctance to talk about her exceptional ability.

The second incident happened in 1971, before mobile phones were available and technology such as television remotes and telephone answering machines were just beginning to catch on. By that time I had married, was mother to three children and was also newly separated from my husband.

On a summer Sunday, my kids and I were driving down I-79 South in my Volkswagen Beetle from New Kensington to my parents' home in Waynesburg, Pennsylvania, a few hours away.

"Knock three times on the ceiling if you wa-ant me, twice on the pipes if the answer is no-oh-oh-oh!" I sang along with my enthusiastic kids in the back seat: Marion, fourth grade going on forty; Stephen, second grade precocious merry-maker; and Cara, first-grade lover of the world.

The sky was clear, the day bright. I was in no hurry to get there because my folks were at a birthday celebration a few towns from where they lived. I had a key to their house and we were staying overnight. Although the kids knew their grandparents wouldn't be home until much later, they were eager to hop out of the car and check out the goldfish pond in the back yard. We still had nearly an hour to go.

The game "I Spy" had replaced the singing while we rode. As I waited for the next question, I saw smoke pouring from the engine at the rear of the car. Seeing the dark smoke in my rear view mirror, I panicked knowing that the children sat perilously close to the Volkswagen motor. Aware that an exit was just ahead, I stepped on the gas, hoping to find a safe place to stop and get the kids out. As we approached the exit the smoke thickened into a black curtain, obliterating the road behind. Terrified, I swerved off the ramp and spotted an old gas station across the street. Seeing no cars on the road, I rolled off the ramp directly into the station.

"Get out! Get out!" I shouted, swinging the doors open and pulling the kids from the back seat. Two elderly men carrying fire extinguishers ran toward the smoking inferno on wheels. My heart beat frantically while my frightened children clung to me, watching the men battle the fire. I was grateful that we were safely off the highway, even though it was an outdated gas station miles from our destination.

After the fire was out, I continued to stand there with

my children. The elders, proud of their victory, sat back and waited to see what I would do.

Still shaky, I sure didn't know.

A telephone booth stood near the old building but I had no phone number for the party's location. My folks had no answering machine at their home. Out of desperation I decided I had to do something rather than just stand there with my kids. Even though it was futile, I decided to call the only number I knew—my parents'.

Phone calls made to outside a limited area were billed long distance in those days. My purse contained a credit card but little cash; so, I gathered the few one-dollar bills in my wallet and handed them to the senior behind the ancient cash register. Smiling broadly, he gave back a handful of quarters, dimes and nickels for the pay phone.

Inside the phone booth I pushed a dime through the slot and dialed "O" for operator. When she answered, I gave her the long distance number and waited. She came back telling me the amount to deposit for the first three minutes and I fed most of my coins into the slots. After the last dime jingled to the bottom, I waited dismally, expecting the phone on the other end to ring and ring without answer.

After only one short ring Mom's anxious voice blurted, "Where are you?"

"You're there!" I squealed with relief.

"Are you and the kids all right?" She sounded scared.

"We're okay. The car engine caught fire, but we got out in time."

"Tell me where you are. I'm leaving now to get you."

After she rescued us and we were on the road to their house, I asked her about the party. Did she and Dad go? Had they come home early? Why did she answer the phone by asking where I was?

She wasn't forthcoming with details. Her answers came in nods, shrugs and diversions to other topics of conversation.

Later I learned that in the midst of partying with old friends twenty miles from where they lived, Mom had suddenly turned to Dad saying she needed to return home immediately. She was troubled by a gnawing premonition that I would be calling for help. Over my skeptical father's objections, she insisted on heading home to receive my call! Reluctantly, he surrendered the car keys and agreed to ride home later with a friend.

By comparing the time it had been when smoke spewed from our engine to the time it had been when Mom left the party, I realized she *knew* we would need rescue at least a full hour before the smoke appeared.

Something beyond my comprehension had been at work, either within or through my mother. That realization filled me with awe and wonder.

In a stream of consciousness, I remembered the first time Mom's action inspired me with awe and wonder. I had not yet turned six years old. We were standing together outside our house.

My young mother pushed a small spade into the black earth. I stood nearby holding a packet of flower seeds in my five-year-old hand. Opening a shallow hole in the ground, she said, "See, this is our part, sweetheart. Our job is to dig a hole and plant the seeds."

She opened the packet, placed a few seeds in my hand and gestured for me to drop them into the fresh soil. After I had finished peeling the last seed from my moist palm, she said, "Okay. Now we cover them lightly with soil so they can grow." Then she brushed some dirt onto the seeds and invited me to finish the job.

"Now that we've planted the seeds, it's our job to give them water and keep weeds from crowding them." She handed me a small pail containing water, which I dribbled over the loose soil. "Now, God does the rest," she added.

I stood staring at the ground. "Is He doing something right now?" I asked.

"Yes He is." she answered. "In several days you'll begin to see proof of God's power and love.

"What's He doing?" I questioned.

"He's giving life to the seeds so they can grow." She said. "The way He does it is a mystery to us."

"Why can't He do it right now? Why do we have to wait?" I asked, impatiently.

"He probably could do it right now," she said looking at the freshly dug soil. "But if He did…then we wouldn't have our part to do. Remember, our job is to water the seeds and protect them. We do our part and God does His."

"How many days?" I asked.

"I don't know the answer to that, honey," Mom said smiling. "God works in His own time. But you'll get an answer to the question you asked earlier this morning." She looked into my face with wide eyes and raised eyebrows. "Remember your question?"

"Yeah. 'How do we know there's a God if we can't see or touch Him?'"

"Uh-huh," she nodded. "Be patient, sweetheart. Your answer will come in several days—when God decides."

Mom had started teaching me to read when I was four. Recently I'd been attempting to read children's Bible stories from a book given to me by my Catholic grandmother. For days I'd been at Mom's heels riddling her with questions about Jesus and God.

Dad's family was Russian Orthodox; Mom's, Roman Catholic. To avoid religious disputes between their families, my parents had chosen a justice of the peace to marry them. We didn't attend church but I had seen different images of Jesus in the homes of my grandparents and our next-door neighbor. They all showed a man with long hair but each image looked like a different person to me.

My Catholic grandmother had further confused me by explaining that Jesus died for our sins. She said I must pray to Him. That pushed me beyond my limit of understanding and imagination!

It was bad enough I couldn't see God and didn't know for sure where He was. Now I should pray to Jesus? (To me, the Russian Orthodox picture of Jesus in Grandma Rodavich's bedroom was spooky!) Was Jesus another God? What did "He died for our sins" mean?

Mom chose her own way to open my mind and heart to a spiritual God without indoctrinating me to religion or church dogma. Rather than teach me prayers to recite, she prayed daily in her own words to "God, our heavenly Father" before our evening meal. Except for the giving-thanks part, she changed the content of her prayers daily to include what was happening in our lives, in our neighborhood and in the world. Watching her pray and listening to her words had kindled my curiosity about God. She quelled my anxiety about Jesus by explaining that He was the Son of God who came to Earth to teach us about God's love and power. People who didn't believe his teachings killed him. After he died, his teachings about God spread throughout the world. Then people started praying to Jesus the same as praying to God.

She assured me that it was okay for me to pray to God.

When the seeds we had planted and watered sent tiny sprouts through the soil, I was convinced that God was making it happen. Then buds appeared and later blossomed into glorious pink flowers. Of course I had seen flowers growing in our neighborhood before, but until we planted those seeds, I had not connected their blooming process with God. To me those pretty flowers were awesome proof of His wondrous magic and power!

God, whom I could not see or touch, became real to me. Nobody had to teach me to pray after that. I just did. When I was troubled or wanted something (like a bike), I'd talk to God in my own words with the belief that He was listening.

Mom was sixteen and Dad was twenty-three when they married. I was born less than a year later and remained their only child for three years until Rodney was born. Three years later baby Stevie completed our family. In spite of her youth, Veronica was a wise and excellent teacher. She inspired me to think and also to love. Her way of teaching me about God is an example of her skill.

The third clairvoyant event I witnessed happened when I was forty-five. I had been divorced, remarried, and was teaching high school English. In addition to my three teenage children, I had three young stepchildren who came on weekends. My life was running at full speed. This sad event brought it to a hard stop.

My youngest brother, Steve, was having a small lump in his neck biopsied at the local hospital. I sat in the waiting room with Steve's wife, Donna, Mom and brother Rod. The four of us had agreed that the biopsy would reveal nothing more than a harmless cyst. Both Mom and I had a history of benign cystic breasts. Those small lumps had been tested repeatedly and diagnosed as harmless genetic inconveniences. We naturally assumed that Steve's small growth was a similar inconvenience.

Adding support to our assumption was the fact that Steve had no discomfort from the growth. His regular workouts at the gym kept him fit and muscular. We were so confident of a favorable outcome that the five of us had planned ahead to have lunch at a favorite restaurant when the procedure was over.

During our wait we chatted, leafed through magazines and chuckled at funny pictures and cartoons. I felt at ease and thought the others did as well. Suddenly without warning, a volcanic sob erupted from deep within my mother! People seated on the opposite side of the room reacted to the sound. Mom doubled over. Sobs wracked her body and tears gushed from her eyes.

We embraced her, handed her tissues, gave her water, made every attempt to soothe her. Our efforts were wasted. Her sobs were unstoppable. We tried getting her to her feet but she didn't have the strength to stand on her own.

Rod and I held her up between us and half carried her outside for some air. Donna, looking stiff and terrified, remained behind for the doctor. I steeled myself to keep from crying.

Mom's loud sobs subsided after we sat outside for a while, but she couldn't stop her tears. I asked what had happened to her, even though I didn't want to know. Rod likely had the same feeling. She shook her head repeatedly. The only words she managed to say were, "Take me back in."

My legs felt like iron pillars as we walked her into the building. Once inside the waiting room, I noticed Donna's red, bloodshot eyes. "Are you all right, Mom?" Donna asked weakly, knowing full well she wasn't.

We helped Mom into a chair, where she sat crying softly, catching her tears in wadded tissue.

For about fifteen minutes we waited with little to say. I felt numb. The surgeon finally entered and escorted us to a private room.

He stood looking at the floor. "It's on days like this that I hate my job," he said.

"What are you saying?" asked Rod. Color drained from his face.

Mom wailed in agony. Donna and I burst into tears.

"Your brother has terminal cancer," the doctor said softly. Tears came to his eyes.

"How can you be so sure of your diagnosis?" Rod snapped. "Doesn't the specimen have to go to pathology first?" Angrily he added, "Are you a pathologist or do you like to play God with words like *terminal?*"

The surgeon reached for a tissue and dabbed his own eyes. "Of course I'll send it to the lab, but I don't need a pathologist to identify that cell. My sister died of the same cancer. When I see that malicious cell through a microscope, I recognize it as though it were the back of my own hand."

Donna and I huddled with Mom and sobbed loudly.

Tears filled Rod's eyes. He blew his nose and took a moment to gain his composure. "How terminal?" he asked.

"Months, is my guess," the surgeon replied softly, "not years."

We stood trying to realize what had just been said.

After a long pause Rod asked solemnly, "Isn't there che-motherapy or radiation that can kill it?"

"No," the doctor responded. "We can't stop it from spreading. We don't even have a means of slowing it down."

Our brother Steve died fourteen months later.

Reliving this event still fills me with sadness, even though I mourned the loss of my brother many years ago. I offer this account as more evidence of Mom's precognition. She didn't say it, but it was obvious to us that she *knew* the surgeon's fatal prognosis well before he entered the waiting room.

* * *

The how and why of these incidents continue to puzzle me. I've wondered if I might have inherited some of my mother's ability. I have not. Witnessing her clairvoyance validated extrasensory perception for me. It also increased my openness to spiritual possibilities.

Perhaps it was that mindset of acceptance and openness that enhanced my spiritual connectivity. Admittedly, I use the words "spiritual connectivity" as conjecture; for, in truth, I can't know for sure why or how my mystical interludes happened. What I do know, and find remarkable is this: though I was surprised by those unexpected and unexplainable events, I was never frightened by them or of them.

While I am not clairvoyant, I have had the experience of writing and also speaking words that seemingly came from an unknown source, as will be revealed in the stories ahead. Each of the ten events I detail in this book is as intense and real to me now as it was when it occurred. I have replayed each one in my mind many, many times searching for answers.

If you have experienced mystical interludes in your life, you've probably faced the same unanswered questions I have: *What made it happen? What does it mean? Will it happen again?*

The first two accounts in the upcoming chapter, "Experiencing God," unlike others in this book, generated no questions. Rather, they illuminated my young heart and mind with love and faith, the enduring mainstays of my existence.

The first narrative, "Gratitude," gives rise to the second, "Forgiveness." They are about my receiving answers to prayers when I was less than nine years old. I was a confused child praying in earnest, trying to make sense of my changing world.

In the 1940s there was no television to offer happy endings for my situation. Nor were there video games to distract me from seeking answers by praying. I sometimes wonder if the outcome would have been the same had I been that same child living in today's world. I like to believe it would.

In the wake of these events, my faith increased, my fear dissolved, and my spiritual openness began to bloom, enabling me to fearlessly receive the mystical interludes that were to follow.

EXPERIENCING GOD

One: Gratitude

1945

A Protestant minister once told me, "Until you've had a personal experience with God, you don't really believe in God; you believe only in the *idea* of God."

* * *

"Stop your nagging!" Daddy shouted.

I awoke and rubbed my eyes. It was dark outside. I knew my dad had come home drunk again.

"Then stop your drinking and come home to your family!" My mother was crying.

"Oh, for Chrissake! Do I have to listen to this again?" His words were slurred.

I sat up in bed and listened.

"You try staying home with three kids, cleaning, cooking, and changing diapers all day!" Mom whined. "Then at night not knowing where your husband is or when he's coming home!" She blew her nose. "I'm sick of it!"

This wasn't new to me, waking up at night and listening to their fights.

"Goddammit Vern! Stop your belly-achin'! What the hell do you think I do all day? I work like a dog, that's what!" I heard his shoes hit the floor with a loud thump. "When I come out of the mine after puttin' in overtime, me and my buddies go out for a few drinks. I need to blow off steam!"

"Blowing your hard earned money on booze is what you're doing!"

"Shut the hell up!" he screamed.

"Go ahead! Wake the kids and the whole neighborhood!" Mom shrieked in a loud whisper.

I was six years old and miserably awake in bed. Pulling a blanket over my head, I prayed that God would make them stop fighting. I had prayed for those fights to end many times before.

We lived in a coalmining village owned by the corporation for which Dad labored long, stressful hours underground. Mom was a dark-haired, dark-eyed beauty of twenty-three, practically imprisoned in our "company" house. She had no car and no diversion with the exception of having conversations with a kind neighbor next door. The cliques of older women in the coalmining patch ignored her.

The fights that woke me up at night had been getting louder, meaner, and scarier. What happened months later was no surprise. Mom left Dad. Having no way to provide for us, she left my brothers and me as well.

It happened on my first day in second grade. Returning from school, I was surprised to find a babysitter with my brothers; Rodney, four and Stevie, fifteen months old. When Dad came home a while later, the girl handed him a letter. She left and I watched him walk slowly toward the stairs as he read. I followed.

After going up a few steps he stopped, turned slowly and sat down. The look on his face was one I had never seen before. Thinking he might be sick, I ran up the steps and hugged him. I felt sad and frightened.

Dad hugged me tightly. "Mommy left us," he said. "She's not coming back."

I don't think I believed him.

Later, he packed our belongings, explaining that we were moving in with Aunt Emily and Uncle Raddy.

"Somebody has to take care of you and your brothers while I'm at work," he said. Aunt Emily, who had no children of her own, lived in a small town close by and within walking distance of an elementary school.

I wanted to refuse! I wanted to shout, *I WANT TO STAY HERE! WHAT IF MOMMY COMES BACK AND WE'RE GONE? SHE WON'T KNOW WHERE TO FIND US!* That's what I would have said. But the sad look on my father's face froze my tongue.

I remember three things about that first night at our new "home": the house smelled of fried onions and cigarette smoke; I slept on an old couch in the room between the kitchen and bathroom; and Dad went out that night after we were "settled," probably to drink with his buddies.

Before I started at my new school, Aunt Em emptied drawers and cupboards to make room for us. To avoid having to "fool with" my long hair (which Mommy either braided or fixed in "Shirley Temple" curls) she sent me for a permanent at Sally's Beauty Shop across the street.

I sat in the parlor chair crying with seemingly hundreds of hot metal clamps attached to my head. The clamps not only burned my scalp, they were so heavy my neck wobbled under their weight. When the torture ended, my hair was a ball of frizz. Not only was I sporting the first afro in 1946, my hair was "fooling-with" proof! There was no way Aunt Em could possibly get a comb or brush through it!

At school I was a pariah. Nobody wanted to get close to the strange new kid who looked so queer. That's because my clothing was sometimes even more outrageous than my hair. If there wasn't a clean white blouse to go with a plaid skirt because she hadn't washed clothes, my aunt forced me to wear any top she found—even though polka dots next to plaid caused vertigo.

Looking at myself in a mirror was shocking. I didn't recognize me. Within a few weeks I had changed from a well-groomed, happy, high-achieving first-grader into a disheveled, miserable, non-achieving second grader.

My brothers fared even worse. Four-year-old Rodney was frail. For some reason, his thin legs looked purplish. They hurt him at night, causing him to kick in his sleep. From my couch outside his room, I often heard his legs pounding the mattress. When he misbehaved during the day, Aunt Em, with her hair-trigger reactions, often slapped him across his bare legs, leaving white handprints.

She fed fifteen-month-old Stevie from her dinner plate, foods like fried pork chops, buttered and salted mashed potatoes, beans, and cottage cheese. When he became constipated, she gave him enemas.

For enemas, my aunt liked to wait until Rodney and I were asleep. Stevie's screams would usually wake me up and I'd cry. Aunt Em would yell at me from the other room. Sometimes Uncle Raddy, who must have thought enemas were necessary, came in and soothed me until I cried myself to sleep.

My worst agony was whenever Aunt Em punished one of my brothers. She'd smack Rodney across his legs or smack Stevie's little fingers for picking up something of hers. He would bawl and I'd fly at her like a small animal, pounding her belly or back with my fists. She'd retaliate by grabbing me by the hair or slapping my face or both.

As extra punishment, she put me to work scrubbing the wainscoting on the lower section of walls in one room.

"There's dirt in those cracks," she said. "You should be able to get in there with your fingers and clean it out. If it doesn't look clean when I inspect, you'll have to do it over again. Get busy!"

That was the beginning of my servitude. Oh, how I remember swollen fingertips, not to mention hands burning from hot water and strong soap. Even so, I preferred scrubbing the wainscoting to scrubbing the kitchen floor on my hands and knees. When I neared the refrigerator with my wet rag, a jolting shock would run through my hands and arms, stunning and frightening me.

You might wonder why my dad didn't step in and rescue us from such treatment. For one thing, he wasn't around very often. Sometimes we didn't see him for days at a time. He left for work in the morning while we slept and didn't get home at night until after we were asleep in bed. I'd worry that he was getting drunk again and prayed that God would bring him home safe.

Sometimes Dad came straight home to have dinner with us. On those days Aunt Em's personality changed. In preparation she'd offer us sweets and clean us up using kind words and smiles. She would forewarn me not to complain or look sad in Dad's presence. "And don't ask him questions about your mother. She broke his heart! He can't take much more."

Then she'd threaten, "If you kids make him even sadder, he might leave you just like your mother did."

Her warnings paralyzed my tongue and nearly stopped my heart. I loved my dad so much! I didn't want to make him sad. And I sure didn't want him to leave!

Night after night I cried myself to sleep, hoping and praying that Mom would return to us. I wondered why God had not been answering my prayers. Was it because I was angry? Was I being a bad girl? Was God even listening?

Although Aunt Em's warning terrified me, one evening I got Daddy alone for a moment.

"Aunt Em's mean to us," I said.

"Don't talk like that," he replied angrily. "She took you and your brothers in and she takes good care of you. Where'd we be without her?" I felt a tight knot in my stomach and couldn't answer.

Uncle Raddy didn't know about her treatment of us, either. He usually got home from work after we had eaten dinner and were in our pajamas playing quietly on the floor.

If Mom sent us cards or letters, we didn't get them. I questioned Aunt Em about her. Did she know where our mother was? Did she ever hear from her?

Aunt Em would bark at me, "No! I don't ever want to hear from your mother. She's nothing but a WHORE!"

The word *whore* was one that my aunt used as a name for my mother. To my mind, she was calling Mommy a *horror*. That made sense knowing how Aunt Em felt about things.

On a day-to-day basis, bedtime was misery for me and probably for my younger brothers as well. Reliving the daily turmoil at school and home filled me with agony. I'd thrash around on my lumpy couch trying to shake it off. Then I'd think of Mommy, remembering her face, the sound of her voice, the touch of her hands as she bathed me, or her scent when she hugged me. My pain would turn to hopeless grief. I'd pray to bring myself out of it, begging God to work His power and bring Mom back. At the same time I wondered if He was listening.

One day Aunt Em told me to answer the ringing telephone. I heard my mother's voice say my name! I cried out "MOMMY!"

Aunt Em rushed forward, snatched the phone from my hand and shouted into the receiver, "Nobody here wants to talk to you! You left!" Grabbing a handful of my hair and yanking my head back, she screamed, "Here's what your daughter thinks of you!" Pulling my hair even harder, she whispered in my ear, "Tell her she's a whore!"

"I love you, Mommy!" I shouted. Aunt Em, now out of control, kept the pressure on by jerking my head back harder and harder until I gasped, "You're a horror!"

"Don't call here again!" Aunt Em screeched and slammed down the receiver.

Afterward she stormed around the house cussing under her breath as if somebody had assaulted her.

I'm sure I cried. Though it's the feeling I remember most. It was an indescribable, sinking *awful*.

To help myself fall asleep I prayed fervently hoping God was listening. I prayed that Mommy would come back and rescue us. I prayed that she and Daddy would get back together so we could be a happy family. I prayed to be stronger. I prayed for my brothers. Sometimes I prayed to stop crying. I prayed with all my heart.

Summer following second grade brought a miracle to our lives. It must have been on a Sunday because Uncle Raddy was home and Dad was out somewhere. I remember thinking something was unusual that morning. Aunt Em had bathed and dressed us in our good clothes.

"Are we going somewhere?" I asked. Those were the only times we ever wore our "good" clothes.

"No. I'm just tired of looking at you in your play clothes." She didn't look happy.

After we were dressed, I kept waiting for something more. I wondered, *Is Uncle Raddy going to take us somewhere? Is company coming?* I asked if we could go outside and play but the answer was, "Not in your good clothes."

I got out a coloring book and crayons. Rodney and Stevie played on the floor with some toys. Uncle Raddy sat in his chair, as usual, smoking his cherry pipe and reading. Aunt Em busied herself in the kitchen.

Our living quarters were on the second floor. The room we were in opened on one end to stairs leading down to the front door. My brothers and I played away from the steps at the room's far end. Hearing the front door open, I looked up wondering who was coming. Uncle Raddy didn't stir from his paper. He didn't even move. Aunt Em didn't come out of the kitchen. Something was strange.

We heard soft, slow footsteps of more than one person coming up the stairs. Rodney and I watched as Daddy appeared around the corner with a big smile on his face. Then MOMMY stepped in from behind him!

Surprise and utter joy propelled me into her arms. I cried, "Mommy! Mommy! You're back! Are you gonna stay with us? Are you gonna take us with you? Mommy, I love you!"

Rodney beside me cried, "Mommy, Mommy!" We wept and clung to her. She cried and hugged us, covering us with kisses.

Although I didn't notice, I imagine my dad had some tears in his eyes. Little Stevie watched from the floor with no recognition. Uncle Raddy smiled, rose and greeted my mom with a hug then headed into the kitchen.

After we calmed down, Dad took us into the living room for privacy. He told us he and Mom had worked things out. We were going to be a family again. I was so excited I could barely sit still. I wanted to pack my suitcase immediately! To my disappointment, he explained that we had to remain with Aunt Em and Uncle Raddy for a while longer until we had our own place to live.

I was disappointed but my happiness prevailed.

Daddy and Mommy and me and my brothers! The five of us together again! My family! Mom said she missed us very much and promised she'd never, ever leave us again.

"I know one thing for sure," she said hugging and kissing us, "I can't live without you!"

After a few hours, Dad explained that he had to take Mom back to where she was temporarily staying. Before they left, she promised to come back each week until we found a place to live.

During the days that followed, I lived in excited anticipation for Mom's visits. We went for walks or to the playground. Sometimes she bought us ice cream at the soda counter in the drug store. I couldn't wait for time to pass until we could move away as a family. Days seemed even painfully longer as I yearned for the future.

Every night, I prayed for Daddy to find a place for us to live *quickly*. Then I prayed for time to pass *quickly*.

One particular night as I tried to settle into sleep after praying, a thought emerged like a light inside my head.

God had answered my prayers!

Mommy is back with us. She loves us. She and Daddy love each other. We are a family again! Everything I had prayed for was happening! God *had* heard my prayers and *answered!!*

Flushed with joy and amazement I sat up, wanting to jump off my couch and shout my news for all to hear! Instead, I took a deep breath, placed my hands over my heart, and cried silently.

This time I cried from sheer happiness.

Feeling good, I lay down to sleep whispering, "Thank you! Thank you! Thank you, God!"

Looking back it's clear to me that in addition to "experiencing" God that night, I felt, deep *gratitude* for the first time in my life. That precious insight opened me to a perpetual source of hope.

EXPERIENCING GOD

Two: Forgiveness

1946 – 1947

"We have something to tell you," Dad said with a smile. He held Stevie on his lap while Mom sat on the sofa beside him looking down at her hands. I couldn't tell if she was happy or sad. Rodney and I were sitting on the carpet in front of the couch looking up at them expectantly. Aunt Em and Uncle Raddy had gone out. We had the house to ourselves.

"Yes?" I squealed. "What is it? What is it?"

"What is it?" mimicked five-year old Rodney, clapping his hands.

"We have a place to live!" Dad said, wide eyed.

"Where? When can we move in?" I asked, bouncing up and down.

"Well, we need a place that's close to your school…and Uncle Raddy needs to rent out his apartment next door…so we'll be moving there in about three weeks!" He ended with a big smile as though it were the best news in the world.

"What?" I asked, my heart in my feet. The apartment next door was located under the same roof as Aunt Em! "We won't be moving a-*way?*" I groaned and looked into Mom's eyes. She glanced quickly at Dad then returned her gaze to her hands.

"Mommy, I thought we were going to move AWAY from here, maybe back to our old house," I pleaded, hoping she could intervene.

Dad intercepted, "We'll move *away* someday, but not now. We're going to move next door first."

"Isn't there someplace else we can move to?" I pouted.

"No, honey, there isn't. Not for now," he said with finality. "You don't want to change schools again…or move away from your friends, do you?"

I wondered what friends he was talking about but didn't say anything.

"School's starting in a month or so. By then we'll be in our new place and we'll be a family again! It'll be fine, you'll see." He reached over and took Mom by the hand. She looked at him and smiled.

Nodding her head she said, "We'll be together, sweetheart. It'll be fine."

The last thing I wanted was to live close to Aunt Em! Swallowing my disappointment, I told myself that living beside her with my family was better than living with her *without* Mommy.

For a little more than three weeks I counted the days and waited impatiently, all the while telling myself that having Mommy back mattered most. I vowed that living next door, I'd steer clear of Aunt Em and be the best girl I could be.

We finally moved in. The second-floor apartment, freshly plastered and painted, consisted of a roomy kitchen and a large central living room connecting two bedrooms, a bath, and a doorway to steps leading down to the front entrance.

My brothers and I slept in a large bedroom at the rear of the house—a hand-me-down double bed for them, a new single bed for me. We were a *family*—Mommy, Daddy, Rodney, Stevie, and me! My younger brothers and I loved each other and shared a close bond. I was a happy girl.

By the end of second grade, my hair had grown and most of the frizz lingered at the ends. Before the beginning of third grade, Mom trimmed the frizz and styled my hair nicely.

I started back to school with eagerness. Mom had bought me clothes I liked and I was pleased with the way I looked in the mirror. I had always loved learning, and our third grade teacher was wonderful. My grades that year started at the top instead of the bottom and the kids in school, even those who wouldn't speak to me the year before, accepted me. I made friends.

In our little town of about a thousand people, everybody walked to school. Our quiet streets were safe to cross or walk along, and nobody's yard was off limits. We played outside freely and safely without parents hovering over us. Nothing was ever planned. Neighborhood kids gathered outside after school, and before long we were racing around for somewhere to hide or sneaking up to a suspicious bush to nab a hider.

We played red rover or army or ball or marbles or something we just thought up. Often we played until it was too dark to see. On weekends my friends and I sometimes packed a bag of sandwiches and explored the hills of a farm nearby. There wasn't a kid in my neighborhood who wasn't a pal.

It was almost a totally happy time. Sadly, troubles with Aunt Em weren't over. She and Mom coexisted in a *cold war* state. Mom had asked me about our stay, but when I started to tell her about Aunt Em's treatment of us, she cut me off. With downcast eyes, she turned away and said, "Never mind."

I knew she'd feel bad if she knew some of the things Aunt Em did. I sure didn't want to make Mommy sad. Afterwards I was careful to avoid the subject with her.

Daddy denied that Aunt Em had mistreated us. Knowing I couldn't talk to either of my parents, I tried hard to forget, or at least not to think about it. As long as the *cold war* lasted, I was able to stay clear of my aunt. But Dad and Uncle Raddy acted as diplomats until *détente* eventually came about. Then the trouble started.

The two apartments were connected at the back by a long, screened-in porch forming a corridor between Aunt Em's kitchen door and ours. I can still hear her footfalls across those wooden planks ending with a rapid tapping on our door.

Mom would call, "Come on in," and Aunt Em would step inside with the air of a shy little girl not wanting to impose.

"When my brother gets home, ask him to come see me. I have something to tell him," she might say with feigned innocence.

Sometimes she tried other ways to pique Mom's ire. One of her favorites was the "innocent" slip of the tongue such as, "Yes, Vernie, those people moved after you left my brother and your kids—I mean when you weren't here." Refusing to engage, Mom gave the appearance of either not hearing or not understanding the hurtful ploys.

I stayed away from my aunt as much as possible. Although Mommy didn't visit her and never invited her to sit down, my detested aunt's visits became more frequent. When I complained to my parents that I wanted her to stay away and leave us alone, they scolded me for my attitude. "Be nice. She's your aunt. We're living in her house. We have to keep peace with her," they would say. Daddy always reminded me that she had taken good care of us.

One day she knocked on the door and asked me to run to the store for her, offering to pay me a nickel. Because Mommy's look told me to comply (and the nickel would buy a cherry popsicle) I agreed. When I returned with her groceries, she insisted that I come in and set the bag on her table. I entered reluctantly. The place looked different—clean and inviting.

"Come into the living room with me," she said, "I want to show you something cute." Curious, I followed her.

There on the mantle next to a small container of water stood the figure of a bird with a long stick of a neck and bright red feathers on its head and tail. The bird's head, which was tilted into the water container as though drinking, bobbed up from the water and in a moment swung back down to as if to drink again. The bobbing movement was ongoing and amusing.

I asked how it worked and where she got it, attempting politeness before leaving. She responded in honeyed tones. Because she was being so kind to me, I assumed she was trying to make things right between us.

Returning from another errand a few days later, I found a note on her kitchen door. It read, "Emily Ann, The door is open. Go in and leave my things on the table." I did as she asked and left quickly.

A day or two afterward, my father called me aside and asked what I had done to the wooden bird on my aunt's mantle.

"Nothing," I said. "Why?"

"You know the bird I'm talking about," he said. Not a question, but a statement. "Somebody broke it."

"What? It wasn't me," I defended.

"How did you know it was there?" he asked.

"Because Aunt Em showed it to me. She took me to her living room and showed it to me."

"Didn't you sneak back into her house one day when she wasn't there?" he asked, eyebrows raised.

"No," I answered.

"Didn't you take groceries into her house when she wasn't there?" he asked.

"Yes. I just put them on the table and left."

"It's always best to tell the truth, Emily Ann," he said. "The bird can be replaced, but you can never take back a lie once it's told."

I was crushed! I couldn't bear the way Daddy was talking to me. How could he not believe I was telling the truth! Feeling powerless and trapped by Aunt Em's lies, I started to cry. "Daddy, I didn't touch that bird! And I didn't sneak into Aunt Em's house!"

He took his handkerchief from his pocket and dabbed my tears. "All the same, honey, she's your aunt who cared for you and you owe her respect. You and I are going over there, and I want you to apologize." He folded the hankie and stuffed it inside the pocket.

"I won't apologize for something I didn't do!" I insisted, desperately hoping he would realize I was telling the truth.

"Just tell her you're sorry something happened to her bird," he said. "Please do it...do it for me."

The pleading in his voice took me over. Feeling twisted up inside, I reluctantly agreed to do it...for him.

Dad tapped on her door and she called, "Come in."

Sitting at her kitchen table crocheting, my aunt smiled at me as though I were the prettiest thing she ever saw. I stared at the floor and walked forward as one approaching a guillotine. Dad waited expectantly at the door.

"I'm sorry something happened to your bird," I said, barely raising my voice above a whisper.

"That's all right, honey," she purred. "It's forgotten already. No need to trouble yourself over it."

Turning back to leave, I caught the pleased expression on Dad's face as he nodded to my aunt. My stomach was filled with nails. I felt like a helpless prisoner. My warden was Aunt Em!

That was only the beginning of more problems.

Later, she "heard rumors" that I had stolen penny candy from the store across the street. After that a neighbor told her he saw me lying in the weeds with several boys. She never approached me with her "service announcements" but went straight to Mom.

"It doesn't look good," she told my mother. "I thought you should know."

Let me be clear. I was a regular kid. Although I played childish pranks on my brothers or friends, I didn't do any of the things Aunt Em accused me of. If I had been seen in the weeds with boys it was because we were in the midst of playing "army," a favorite neighborhood game where we dragged ourselves along the ground preparing to ambush an "enemy."

When Mom came back to us, I had vowed that I would be the best girl I could possibly be. I didn't ever want give her a reason to leave us again. Early on, she taught us never to lie, steal, or cheat. Even though I was tempted at times, I stuck to the rules. (To this day, my face gives me away if I try to fib about something.)

When confronted with my "warden's" reports, I declared my innocence. I think Mommy believed me. Daddy would let it pass as though he believed me, then he'd turn around and warn me not to do anything "like that" in the future.

His mission was to avoid a war with Aunt Em, no matter what. "She's your aunt, and she loves you," he'd repeat. "I want you to be nice to her. Show her respect. After all, she took good care of us when we needed her."

I heard those words over and over again from Dad. Each time he said them, I screamed inside. *I was trying!* All I wanted was to please him and keep peace for Mom and not cause trouble for them!

Why did their happiness depend on *my* being *nice* to Aunt Em? *She* was the one causing trouble, not me! Why was everything *my* fault! Couldn't they see she was making things up about me?

I had feared her. Now I hated her. I hated her more than I ever hated anybody—even Miss Warne, my second-grade teacher who last year looked down her nose at me and scowled as though she were looking at a worm. Having nobody to talk with worsened my burden beyond endurance. I had nowhere to turn, except....

* * *

My second experience with God happened a few days later on a Saturday morning in early fall. My best friend Linda and I, along with Margie and Susie, carried bagged sandwiches on a farmland hike. Crossing a meadow, the girls chatted and frolicked as usual. Their laughter enraged the fury that burned within me. I tried to act carefree, but my friends were not fooled.

Linda said, "Em, what's wrong with you? Don't you feel good?"

Susie followed, "Yeah...what's wrong?"

"I'm okay...just a little sleepy, I guess." They teased me about not getting enough beauty rest and suggested remedies like hugging a teddy bear or sipping warm milk at bedtime. I knew they were kidding but my agitation had overtaken me.

About a hundred yards to the left, I noticed a small grove of tall trees. Feeling drawn to it, I said, "Sorry, I'm just in a bad mood. I need to be by myself for a while." I pointed, "See those trees over there? That's where I'm going. You keep walking, and I'll catch up with you."

They agreed and went on at a slow pace.

Once inside the gathering of trees, I looked up through the branches at the blue sky. On the ground, sunlight dappled the grass and fall leaves. It felt like a holy place, peaceful and serene. I stood still and breathed deeply. After a few minutes, I knelt and prayed.

> *Dear God, I haven't prayed to You in a long time, but I know You're here. You answered my prayers and brought Mommy back. Thank You again. But...I really need Your help now. I'm angry with Aunt Emily for the trouble she causes me and Mommy! Daddy wants me to be nice and treat her with respect. I want to, but... but...I hate her! I hate her for all the bad things she's done to us. I can't get the hate and anger out of me. I think of it all the time—even when I try hard to think of other things. I don't want this miserable feeling...it never goes away, no matter what I do. Please...please...help me. Please tell me how I can get rid of it. Please help me... please tell me what to do.*

I stopped praying as though I had come to the end of a telegram message. Remaining on my knees, I waited for an answer. The fresh morning air and the stillness of the meadow calmed me. With head bowed, I waited...and... waited.

About to give up, I suddenly felt as though a tiny seed had been dropped into my fertile mind. It was the word, *forgive.* "Hearing" it surprised me! It was a word I knew but hadn't thought about much. I whispered it, "forgive." The word had a calming effect. "Forgive," I said out loud. A feeling of peace came over me.

I'd asked God for an answer and the word *forgive* filled

my mind. Even though I wasn't sure of its full meaning and didn't know how to do it, I believed God had given me His answer! I trusted it would work somehow.

Gratitude filled me the way it had when Mom returned. I thanked God profusely. My anguish gone, I bounced to my feet and ran to catch my friends.

Little did I know how that prayer would change my life.

During the following days, I went around asking adults to tell me what it meant to "forgive," starting with my mother.

> "To forgive means to let go of anger or pain that somebody has caused you," she said.
>
> "Does 'forgive' mean to 'forget' about what a person did to you?" I questioned.
>
> "Not exactly," she said thoughtfully. "You probably can't *forget* what somebody did, but if you forgive them, the memory of what they did won't bother you anymore."
>
> I couldn't imagine a time when the memory of what Aunt Em had done to us wouldn't "bother" me anymore. That was impossible! Still, I had to keep trying to do what God told me.

Our walk to school took us past the Presbyterian Church. It wasn't a church I attended but Pastor McCready was a well-loved friend to most of us in our town. On the way home one day, I walked into the empty church calling, "Is anybody here?" After a few seconds, I heard footsteps.

He approached. "Hi there, Emily," the pastor said with a big smile. "What can I do for you?"

"I want to ask a few questions," I said. Reverend McCready was a man in his forties, medium height and weight with dark hair parted on the side. His round face was soft featured, his brown eyes glowed with kindness and love.

"Okay, come into my office," he said leading the way. He sat down and directed me to a chair facing his. "What are your questions, Emily? I'll answer them if I can," he said cheerfully.

"I want to know more about what 'forgive' means," I said. "I know it means to let something go. Like…if someone lies to you or hurts you…you don't try to hurt them back. You just…ignore it and let it go. My question is…what if you can't *forget* what they did to you? What if when you think about it, you get angry and feel hate all over again? How can you forgive someone if you can't stop thinking about what they did?"

"I see," he replied slowly. "Good question." A pause. "Well, the key to forgiveness is love." Another pause. "You must fill your heart with love, first." Looking into my eyes, "Do you have love in your heart, Emily?"

"Yes, for Mommy and my family," I said.

"Good. Then you know what love feels like."

"Yeah."

"Do you think you can have love in your heart for the person you want to forgive?" he asked.

"I never tried it." I said.

"Do you believe in Jesus?" he asked.

"I don't think so," I said, "but I believe in God. I know God answers prayers."

"Well, Jesus was the son of God who lived on this earth a long time ago," he said.

"Yes, I know. Jesus was nailed to a cross and died. I've seen pictures and statues."

"Do you know what he said before he took his last breath? He prayed to his Father, God, to forgive his enemies. He said, "Forgive them Father for they know not what they do."

"Why'd He ask God to forgive them? Shouldn't He be the one to forgive them?" I asked.

"He asked God to forgive them because what they did to Him was the same as doing it to God."

"I don't understand," I said.

"You love your brothers, right?" he asked.

"Yeah." I answered.

"A person who hurts your brother also hurts you, making you upset, right?"

"Yes."

"By asking God to forgive, Jesus was asking his Father not to be upset with the people who were hurting him," he said.

"Okay," I said, understanding.

"Jesus was also letting everyone know that He had already forgiven his enemies. By saying those words, Jesus taught us about forgiveness."

"How's that?" I asked.

"Well, it's because Jesus taught that we should love our fellow man. That means everybody—even our enemies. Asking God to forgive the people who were killing Him showed that Jesus practiced what He preached. He loved his enemies and was able to forgive them."

"It's pretty hard to love *every*body, especially our enemies," I quipped. "Do you love everybody?" I thought about movies my friends and I watched showing ugly Japanese soldiers torturing and killing our soldiers and gunning them down in the air.

"To the best of my ability," he answered.

"What about the Japs who killed our soldiers in the war?" I asked.

"Ah, yes. Good question. I don't love war," he explained, "but I don't hate the Japanese people. They're just like us."

"How do you mean?" I asked. I'd *never* thought the Japs were just like us!

"Well, their soldiers, like ours, had no choice but to follow orders. Every soldier killed, whether American or Japanese, was somebody's brother, father or husband."

"I guess so," I said, trying to imagine civilian Japanese families.

"To forgive, Emily, you must think about the hurtful situation from all sides."

"How do you mean?"

"Do you think Japanese people see us as cruel and wicked people because we killed their soldiers and bombed their towns?"

"Yeah. Probably they do."

This thought had never come into my head before. "Do you believe Americans are cruel and wicked?"

"No."

"So, which side is right?"

I thought for a few seconds. "I don't know who's right, for sure."

"The war's over now. Our countries are at peace. Do you think the Japanese should keep on hating us Americans?"

"No. They probably do though, just like we hate them."

"The war's over. Shouldn't the hatred be over as well? Each country was doing what it had to do. How long do you think hatred and bitterness should last?"

"I don't know." His questions were making me uncomfortable.

"What might happen if it doesn't come to an end?"

"Probably another war."

"That's right. That's why *forgiveness* is so important. It replaces hatred and bitterness with love and peace."

"Then should we forgive the Japs?" I asked, thinking it was the craziest idea I could imagine.

"We're forgiving the Japanese right now," he said smiling. "Our countries have signed peace treaties."

"Oh," I said, thinking to myself that signing a treaty doesn't stop Americans from hating Japs. Not wanting to disagree I asked, "Why should *we* forgive the Japs *first?*"

"See, Jesus also taught that we should forgive others if we ever want to be forgiven. If we are to follow God's will, it's up to us to take the first step." He added, "Can you see that?"

"Yeah," I said, thinking God told me to take the first step when He said, "Forgive."

"Emily, to forgive we have to love big and think big. If we think small, it's like looking at a large picture through a tiny peephole. We see only a small part of it. When we look at the whole picture as God sees it, that's when we can begin to forgive." He looked at me intently. "Do you understand that?"

"I think so. But how can you *forget?* I mean...are those families who had gold stars in their windows supposed to forget that it was the Japs who killed their loved ones?"

"No, Emily. If American families can look at the big picture they'll see that Japanese families are also grieving for their loved ones killed by war. Seeing the big picture they'll realize it was *war* that made our countries enemies. Soldiers from both our countries suffered and died because of *war*. Families can then begin to forgive."

"Okay, but can they ever forget?" I asked pointedly, thinking he could never convince me that it was possible.

Reverend McCready leaned forward and looked deep into my eyes. "We Americans won't ever *forget* that our loved ones fought and died in the war with Japan, but we can remember without *hating* the Japanese. Do you know why?"

"Why?" I asked.

"We can see the 'big picture.' We realize that the Japanese are just like us. Americans are not by nature killers, and neither are the Japanese. It was *war* that made us enemies. It was *war* that caused bloodshed and hatred."

"So we blame the killing on war?" I asked. I could feel a little *ah-ha* going on in my head.

"That's what war does." He answered. "It's important for both countries to see that."

"You mean…America's families never forget about the *war* that caused their men to die, but they stop hating the Japs for it."

"Yes." He smiled at me. "Learning to forgive is very important to our lives, Emily."

"It's not easy to do," I said with downcast eyes. I had no war to blame for Aunt Em's lies and abuse.

"No, not at first. It's worth all the effort that's needed, Emily."

"I guess so," I answered, not sure I believed it.

"Know this," he said, getting to his feet, "forgiveness removes the sting from a bad memory and dissolves hatred and anger. What could be worth more than that?"

"Thanks," I said, getting to my feet. "Thank you very much, Reverend, for answering my questions." I walked toward the door, feeling as though my mind had been stretched to its limits—maybe beyond.

"Anytime, Emily. My door's always open." he said smiling his kind smile.

I replayed the pastor's explanation in my mind day after day.

Then I started trying to forgive Aunt Em.

First, I tried feeling love for her. That didn't work.

Then I thought of people in her life who loved her, like my Grandma. I tried to picture Aunt Em as a little baby in

Grandma's arms, then as a little girl going to school and growing up and marrying Uncle Raddy. Little did I know that when I became curious about my aunt's life, I had taken my first step away from the "peephole" and moved toward the "big picture."

Dad told me Aunt Em was the oldest of his sisters in a family of eleven—eight girls and three boys. When she was old enough to dress herself, Grandma put little Aunt Em to work with every task she could handle. Each time a new baby came, my little-girl aunt had more and more work to do.

Before she was my age, Aunt Em was changing diapers, washing dishes, and scrubbing floors. Her responsibility of caring for younger brothers and sisters left her no time for friends or play or even homework. She was absent from school a lot and her grades were below passing. That gave her cause to drop out of school at the end of third grade, never to return.

I asked Daddy if she ever moved away from her home and got a job. He said she didn't leave home until she married my uncle. I asked how she met him if she never went anywhere and had no friends. He told me Uncle Raddy had visited my grandfather one day and saw Aunt Em. Although Uncle Raddy was at least eleven years older, he took an interest in her and asked Grandpap if he could take her as his wife. Grandpap said yes, so Aunt Em and Uncle Raddy got married.

The big picture started to take shape. Looking at the other side and trying to see things through my aunt's eyes, I wondered how I'd be if I couldn't go to school, had no friends, had to do housework and take care of babies and little kids all the time. It was no wonder Aunt Em didn't have babies of her own. She probably didn't want kids because of all the hard work they caused her.

She'd probably let us move in with her, not because she wanted to take care of us, but because my dad needed a place for us to stay. Putting me to work scrubbing floors and washing dishes was "normal" to her because that's what she did when she was my age. My heart softened as I started to see the "big picture."

I thought about trying to love her again. I wasn't ready to go that far. I wondered how much Dad and Uncle Raddy loved her. They were nice to her but I hadn't seen either of them give her a hug or kiss her on the cheek. I sure hadn't ever done it. The whole time we lived there I fought against her.

Then I thought about the lies she told about me. Hatred stirred. Quickly switching to look at the other side, I decided she probably didn't like me. I knew she didn't like Mom. The lies she told gave her a way to hurt both of us at the same time. But that was no excuse! I couldn't see how looking at the other side could help me feel any better about her lies.

I was haunted by the fact that God had answered my prayer. Reverend McCready had taught me what it meant to forgive and had even given me a blueprint for how to *do* it. I doubted if it was possible for me. I hadn't been able to muster up enough love for her and I couldn't get past her painful lies.

At the same time I couldn't just ignore God's answer. Each night in bed I pondered ways to overlook my aunt's lies. I'd tell myself that if Jesus could forgive people for killing Him, I should be able to forgive Aunt Em just for lying! In my head I'd recite, "Sticks and stones can hurt my bones, but words will never hurt me." Then I usually fell asleep without a solution.

October was coming to an end. One night after going round and round with my thoughts, I managed to devise a plan.

The next day I got permission from Susie's mom to let me pick some mums from her garden. With flowers in hand, I headed straight to Aunt Em's door while carefully rehearsing what I would say. Hearing my knock, she called, "Come on in."

There she sat at her kitchen table playing solitaire and smoking a cigarette. Looking at me skeptically she said, "Emily Ann…is something wrong? What do you want?"

I walked in and held out the golden flowers. "I picked these for you, Aunt Em."

She eyed me suspiciously.

"I…never thanked you for taking care of me and my brothers," I continued. "You…probably didn't want to take care of us three kids…but you did it anyway." Trying hard to feel love in my heart, I took a deep breath, forced a smile and said, "I just wanted to say…thank you."

Catching me off guard, she practically leapt from her chair and pulled me to her! I quickly turned my face to keep from sinking into her soft, bulbous breasts. "Oh, honey, that's so nice of you to say!" She clinched me into a hug and swayed from side to side. Her belly cushioned me like a pillow.

"You're…very welcome," I managed to say.

She snatched the flowers from my hand and set them in a glass of water.

I eased my way toward the door.

"You don't have leave so soon, do you?" She sounded like she wanted me to stay.

As I stood there not knowing what to say or do, she lifted a round lid from a dish on the counter, uncovering a mound of fresh raisin-filled cookies. Then she fetched another glass from the cupboard and headed for the refrigerator to pour me some milk.

Soon I was eating the delicious cookies, sipping milk, and answering her questions about silly things like *Did I have a boyfriend? What was my favorite comic strip? Did I like to play Chinese checkers?* I remember Aunt Em smiling a lot. I probably did, too.

Later I walked across the sun porch with a plate of cookies for my family. The seed of forgiveness had taken root within me.

During the following days and weeks, Aunt Em became a lot nicer—even fun!

Most days after I returned from school, she'd call me over to play Chinese checkers. Then she became curious about the games my friends and I played.

Before long my best friend Linda and I were playing jacks with Aunt Em on her kitchen table. The three of us would have contests to see who could pick up the most jacks at once.

Then she taught me to play canasta. I really looked forward to Saturday night games with Aunt Em and two of my other aunts.

My anger and hatred dissolved, just as Reverend McCready said they would. Forgiveness had bloomed within me, bringing Aunt Em and me together in fun and friendship. I was even able to overlook her lies. They just didn't matter any more.

Forgiveness seemed to change my aunt. Not only was she fun to be with, she even became kind of pretty.

She and my mother got along better, too.

Yes, I even grew to love her.

God had truly answered my prayer! I could *never* have thought of forgiveness on my own. Nor would I have achieved it without the help of Reverend McCready. Forgiveness was the *perfect* answer.

That childhood miracle—*learning to forgive*—has graced my existence with an understanding that has generated life-long blessings for myself and others.

It is my deepest wish that the telling of this story can inspire young people or the parents of young children—or anyone, for that matter—to learn to forgive.

NEAR-DEATH EXPERIENCE

1956

After I forgave Aunt Em, everything seemed to change. For the next few years, my life kept getting better than ever. I became a girl scout, my friends and I took tap dancing classes together, my grades were good, and best of all I was given the thrill of performing a few song-and-dance routines in a community show.

Moving away from Aunt Em and our duplex apartment was a forgotten desire. Moving away from our little town of Carmichaels was the last thing I wanted.

Dad's continuing education in mining landed him a job as assistant mine foreman of the Hubbard Mine in McKeesport, Pennsylvania. We moved there when I was about to enter eighth grade. My unhappy brothers and I sadly bemoaned leaving our good friends and neighborhood.

The kids in my new school seemed like aliens from another planet. The homey, small-town atmosphere had been replaced by one of cold indifference. During recess, instead of playing softball or red rover, students stood around outside on a concrete play area and talked. The girls scattered into small groups. None of them reached out to me.

I gladly walked home for lunch each day, relieved that I didn't have to sit by myself at a table while kids who brought bagged lunches gathered in small groups and excluded me.

My sullenness at school didn't go unnoticed. One morning shortly after I arrived, my teacher, Miss Bales, wrote these words on the chalkboard: "Bloom where you are planted."

I got her message, even if it wasn't meant specifically for me.

Rather than wait for others to approach me, I began extending myself to them. Soon I was in the groove again of having friends and looking forward to school each day. By the end of the school year I loved McKeesport as much as I'd loved our little town of Carmichaels.

By the time I became a senior in high school, Dad had been promoted to mine superintendent and we were living in the superintendent's house provided by the mining company. For the first time we enjoyed the luxuries of spacious rooms, two bathrooms, and even a family room.

The summer following high school graduation was a life changer. My sights were set on college—even though Dad had told me I was on my own if I wanted to continue my education after high school.

"Your two brothers will be the bread winners for their families," he had said. "They'll need a college education, but for you a secretarial position will do. You'll probably marry a good man who'll support you."

But nothing was going to stop me! With or without Dad's help, I'd get a job, save my money and work my way through school. My whole life was ahead just waiting for me to live it!

Giving myself the first two weeks after graduation to wind down and change gears, I cleaned my bedroom, including my closet and all my drawers, much to Mom's delight. I wanted to leave public school clutter behind and make space for the future.

All was well except for my allergies. For years my fingers would itch then swell and blister. Spring brought sinus headaches. Needle tests showed that I was allergic to many foods and certain plants and pollens, so my allergist started me on weekly immunization shots designed to keep me reaction free.

On a Saturday morning in June after my routine visit to the allergist, I felt fatigued, light-headed and chilled. Once home I put on a bathing suit and hurried to the back yard wanting the sun's warmth to soothe me. I dozed almost immediately.

In a short while, my mother roused me, not because I had been too long in the sun, but because my face looked strange to her. When I awoke my ears were ringing and my eyes had swollen almost shut. Soon I realized everything was swollen—lips and tongue, hands, feet, face—everything!

I was surprised by my condition but too dazed to care. Along with the ringing in my ears, I still felt light-headed and exhausted.

"Oh my, Em! This swelling must be related to your allergy shot this morning," Mom said. "Let's get you a cool bath. It'll make you feel better."

Once inside the house, she supported me up the stairs and into the bathtub. My movements were slow and clumsy.

Mom rinsed me down with tepid water then carefully helped me out of the tub, patted me dry and walked me into my warm, non-air conditioned bedroom. All I wanted was a place to rest my head.

Without even attempting to get me into undies or a nightgown, Mom led me to the bed and covered me with a sheet. I closed my eyes and drifted off to sleep again.

Later Mom came in with some water and told me she had called the allergist and described my condition to him. "He said it might be from lying in the sun right after getting the shot. He's hoping you'll sleep it off." His advice seemed plausible because I had never before reacted to an allergy shot.

"He wants you to drink as much water as you can and rest." She held the water to my lips.

Very little made it past my swollen tongue and throat.

Throughout the day the swelling worsened. By the next morning, my body had ballooned to four or five times its normal size. The skin on my arms and legs had split open and a clear fluid oozed from the cracks. The nipples of my breasts were also split and oozing. Mom had placed tall, round ice cream boxes on either side of me and stretched the bed sheet over them to keep the cloth from touching my painful, seeping flesh.

My heartbeat thundered in my ears and I could feel the blood rushing through my arteries and veins. I struggled to breathe.

Wanting to detach from my burning, throbbing body, I shrunk within myself and faded in and out of consciousness.

I recall hearing the distant voice of Doc Harris, our family doctor, saying to my mother, "Veronica, she's critical. Putting her in the hospital is out of the question. She shouldn't be moved…there isn't anything that can be done. She can't swallow, so I can't give her anything by mouth. An injection is too risky…. All we can do is pray."

Later Mom told me she and Doc Harris knelt beside my bed and prayed together. She said Dad made several trips in and out of my room and prayed as well.

The last thing I remember hearing that day was the word "pray." I wasn't conscious again until late the following afternoon. What I experienced in the interim is as vivid to me now as when it happened.

* * *

I found myself sitting on a train traveling through black space. Outside the windows I could see a few tiny stars in the distance sparkling like small diamonds. I knew I was no longer in my bed or on earth, but I was not afraid. The swelling and pain were gone. I felt delightfully alive!

Ten or more women and men were seated in front of me, scattered throughout the passenger car. Each sat alone facing forward without making the slightest sound or movement. The men wore black suits and the women wore dresses in dark shades of blue, brown or purple. Black veils covered the women's heads. Faces were hidden from behind but the passengers felt distantly familiar. I wondered if they had been friends of my parents or grandparents, folks who had treated me kindly when I was younger.

I heard no sound inside or outside the train as we moved through the darkness of space. Time didn't exist. I knew I was in an unearthly realm, but I was unafraid, only curious.

A uniformed man wearing a conductor's hat atop his full head of white hair moved down the aisle toward me. His skin was quite fair and his face beamed, almost glowed with kindness. Love radiated from him as he approached, making me feel that I was under his protection. I trusted him instantly.

"Can you please tell me where this train is going?" I asked. The silent, unmoving passengers gave me the feeling that they were going to a funeral.

"We'll be there soon," he answered gently.

"Can you tell me why these people are so still?" I asked, suddenly wondering if the passengers might not be alive—but dead!

Before he answered I added, "I have a feeling they've died. Have they died?"

During that time in my life I was possessed by a terrifying fear of death, dying, and dead people. Being unafraid among people whom I thought to be dead was *not* something I could conceive!

"Not really," he said, smiling. The train slowed. "Wait here," he said. "I will come back for you."

He returned to the front of the car as the train came to a stop. The passengers rose rigidly, one by one and formed a line at the exit door. I was eager to know where the train had arrived. Looking out the windows, I saw nothing but darkness.

The door slid open soundlessly. The people began leaving, not in a fluid procession, but slowly, each pausing as though waiting to be called by name.

"Is this where I get off?" I called to the conductor, wanting to understand where we were.

He returned and took my hand. The warmth of his Love flowed through me. "You may not leave, Emily," he said lovingly, "but you can see."

I wondered why I was on the train if I wasn't permitted to get off.

He led me to stand behind three or four people at the open door.

Amazing golden LIGHT—LIGHT more brilliant than any light I have ever seen—radiated outside the opening. No matter how far I reach for descriptive words, none can convey it. The LIGHT felt ALIVE! It was both LOVE and harmonious MUSIC! Standing before the LIGHT with the Loving Conductor at my side, I felt swaddled in LOVE so overwhelming, that the memory of it to this day resonates through me and fills my eyes with tears!

I watched each person before me step from the car and disappear, becoming one with the vibrant, loving LIGHT.

As I beheld the astounding brilliance before me, I became aware that I could gaze into it without needing to shade my eyes. The LIGHT seemed omnipresent and endless. Nothing before me was not LIGHT.

In the distance, vaguely outlined in a darker hue of gold stood a cluster of low domed structures similar to the small mud houses of biblical times illustrated in a few of my childhood books. Seeing the houses gave me a feeling that the passengers who had transformed were also merging into a Community within the LIGHT.

I *knew* I was experiencing the hereafter we call Heaven. Overpowering LOVE radiated within me and illuminated everything around me! Everything—Love, Life Energy, Souls, Heavenly Structures, Harmonious Music—everything I witnessed was both *in* the LIGHT and *of* the LIGHT. I was in a Realm far beyond anything my mind could possibly have created. I'm crying as I write this.

Peering to the right outside the opening, I beheld the golden outline of an angelic figure appearing to be male. He stood tall atop the dome of a small house. I watched him spread large, magnificent wings and glide to the "ground" ever so softly and gracefully. I was astonished!

"Look!" I exclaimed to the Conductor. "Do you see that angel? He's a man! I thought all angels were female!" (Later I realized that my thinking had been based on a picture of a beautiful female angel guarding two children crossing a rickety bridge, which my grandmother had hung above my bed. I still have a copy of it.)

"Is that so?" He asked.

I yearned to step off the train and become one with the LIGHT. "Please let me enter," I begged. "I want to stay!"

"Not now, Emily," he said lovingly. "It's not your time. You must return."

The door slowly slid closed.

* * *

I awoke the following afternoon trapped inside my body of throbbing pain. The swelling had subsided considerably, but my heartbeat still boomed in my head. I could barely open my crusted eyelids enough to glimpse Mom at my side. The open cracks in my limbs and nipples still oozed. To make matters worse, the fluid that had seeped during the former day and night had dried and crusted, gluing me to the bottom sheet.

While mom patiently and gently patted me with cool compresses, slowly freeing each inch of me from the cloth, I was feeling the emotional ecstasy from the overwhelming love and the indescribable light/music. I couldn't stop tears from burning their way down my swollen cheeks. I felt that I might burst from glee!

The featureless mask that was my face could not express the smallest hint of my exhilaration. Squinting through swollen lids at Mom's troubled face, I guessed she thought my tears were from pain and misery.

Mom left the room and returned with a roomy lightweight robe, the sleeves of which she had slit open so I could get my swollen arms through. She gently helped me into a sort of sitting position, slipped my arms through the large openings and gently rolled me out of bed. We groped our way to the bathroom.

A peek at my distorted face in the bathroom mirror made me want to laugh. Godzilla, next to me, was a fairytale princess! It was no matter. Joy filled my being! I knew my grotesque, swollen condition would pass and I would be restored. My greatest frustration was that I couldn't sing it out.

Later Doc Harris stopped by with some pills for me to take when I could swallow. He confided his suspicion that I had received an overdose of the immunization shot.

"You're a lucky girl," he added. "People die from such things. I'm frankly surprised that you're still with us."

"I think our prayers were answered," Mom said nodding to him.

"Is that a smile on your face, Emily?" he asked with surprise.

You can't begin to imagine the smile in my heart! I thought.

"I think she's feeling better," Mom answered. "She's been alert since she woke up."

More than you know! I thought.

Unable to talk, I nodded. When I allowed my heavy eyes to close again I saw that radiant light in my head and felt its loving energy. Then I drifted off to sleep. Little did I know there was more to come.

I awoke in the middle of the night. Lying there in silence, I relived my experience, *knowing* I had stood at the doorstep of heaven. Then the questions started: *Did I die then come back to my body? Why wasn't I allowed to stay? Why has this happened to me?*

My certitude began to waver. In 1956 the term *Near-Death Experience* had not been coined. I had never heard of such a thing. Having no words to describe, even to myself, what I had experienced, I wondered if I had hallucinated the event. Other than in Biblical stories or fiction, such things simply did not happen—not in the *real* world!

The fact that my heart was happy while my body throbbed with pain counteracted my doubt. The happiness I felt was not an illusion. It was *genuine!*

Then I wondered why the swelling had overtaken me, and why I had been allowed to see heaven.

I prayed to God for answers.

I waited.

And waited.

Just as I was about to give up and fall asleep, these words strolled through my mind: *When shadows fall athwart thy path, tis God who passes by.*

Again tears burned my swollen skin and dampened my pillow. I repeated the words in my head, vowing never to forget them.

When shadows fall athwart thy path, tis God who passes by. Yes, my sudden illness had been the "shadow athwart my path." God had done more than just "pass by." He embraced me with his Love and allowed me a glimpse of the Divine Light of Heaven!

I *knew* I had not hallucinated! I also knew that my life had been transformed by my new awareness. I understood that love is the essence of life, the holy grail of human existence. Until then I had been consumed by doing well in school, getting a job, saving money for college, building my future and getting ahead. I would continue to work toward my goals, but I would do it with love at the core of my being.

As soon as I could articulate words I told Mom about my "Heaven" experience and the answer to my prayer. She listened to both accounts with sincere acceptance and thoughtfulness.

I asked her if she'd ever heard of the words I received, "When shadows fall athwart thy path, tis God who passes by." She said they sounded like something from a hymn, a religious poem, or maybe a sermon.

"I'm sure I haven't heard or read these words before they came into my mind," I asserted..

"The brain's a tricky thing," she said. "People under hypnosis are able to remember license numbers and things they have no conscious memory of seeing."

Reverend Brown came to visit one day and I asked if he

had ever come across those words in the Bible or hymn or any of his readings. He said he had run across the phrase "athwart thy path" in other contexts but had no recollection of the line I'd given him.

When I was able to leave the house, I visited a library and recruited a librarian to help me search for those words in hymns, poetry, or published pieces of writing, but we could find nothing. Searching for a quote without the Internet was a time-consuming undertaking.

From that point on, I remained on the lookout for the words. In college I majored in English, which required extensive reading of poetry and literature, but I did not find those words in anything I read. I recited them to classmates and instructors as I went through school hoping I could track their origin. Nobody I spoke with could help me.

From 1973 to 1998 I taught high school English. During those years I repeated the line to my colleagues, my students, and also any teachers I met at local, state, and national English conferences. Nobody recognized it.

After the Internet became available, I ran searches for the line almost every year with no result. In 2012 my partner, Jim, ran a search and got a hit!

It was in a blog. The blogger, Patricia Keyser of Huntsville, Alabama, was a second cousin to the author of a poem that contains the line. Here is the beginning of Mrs. Keyser's blog.

Sunday, May 30, 2010
Sharing the Cousin I barely knew

CATHERINE EVELYN COFFEY (1907-2001) was my father's first cousin and the only surviving member of the family to bear the name. She never married and had children, but she did leave a vast number of mysterious and ethereal poems that both reveal and hide who she was. I only met her once, when I was a young teen, and I remain enchanted with my memories of her to this day. In this blog I'd like to share what I know of her and her poetry, and to invite others who knew her to add their memories.

Here is the poem which contains the line I heard in my mind in 1956:

Confidence

When shadows fall athwart thy path,
'Tis God Who Passes By!
Bow down in peace and praise and pray,
And even while you sign,
Remember this, -- Each sorrow is a shadow sweet
tells how near Christ's nailed feet
Are walking by thy side
Then Let Thy Soul Confide!

When I read this poem for the first time, I was struck by how perfectly it answers the question of my 1956 prayer, "Why did this happen to me?"

What is even more relevant is the poem's title. After my near-death experience, I was "confident" that I would be restored to perfect health. And from that day forth, I have been "confident" that love is the essence of life and that life is eternal.

Several months ago I was able to speak on the phone with Patricia Keyser, the blogger. I called her to find more information about the poem. Mrs. Keyser told me that her cousin, Evelyn, was a spinster who lived in Cleveland, Ohio. After Evelyn's death in 2001, one of her close friends gave

Mrs. Keyser a notebook filled with Evelyn's handwritten poems. Until that time Mrs. Keyser didn't know Evelyn wrote poetry.

According to the friend, Evelyn's poems were private. To his knowledge none of the poems had been published. All Mrs. Keyser could say was that the poem had probably been written sometime between 1920 and 2001. Few of the poems in the notebook were dated.

At the time of this writing, Mrs. Keyser's blog has been inactive since the year 2012.*

It seems highly unlikely that in 1956, an eighteen-year-old in McKeesport, Pennsylvania, would have had access to a poem written privately sometime between 1920 and 2001 by a devout spinster in Cleveland, Ohio.

The first line of Evelyn Coffey's poem, which I have carried in my mind and heart from that day to this, has sustained me through many trials. In addition, I have speculated that these two experiences prepared me for other types of mystical interludes to follow.

---

*As data availability has grown, I have continued my search for another possible origin or mention of the poem. Recently I discovered three sources where the poem "Confidence" appears. None of these sources cite the poem's author or even the traditional "anonymous."

February 15, 2012: a funeral page of the Bosma-Renkes Funeral Home Ltd. Website. I spoke to a representative of Bosma-Renkes who checked their library and reported that the poem did not come from them but from a family member. I then contacted the daughter of the deceased to inquire about the poem but she said she had no information regarding the poem.

December 7, 1963: an obituary printed in *The News*, Frederick, Maryland, Page 12, in which the poem "Confidence" appears as it was recited by he Reverend L. J. Summerfield at the funeral of W. Earl Wright.

May 13, 1941: Notre Dame's Religious Bulletin which eulogizes deceased freshman, Jimmie McMichael. It states that after Jimmie's death a verse was found....fastened in his notebook. That treasured verse of his can be a solace to his parents and sisters; can be an answer this side of Heaven to them and to his friends here who prayed so hard for him, and now ask, "But why, out of all of us, did God take Jimmie — the best?" Jimmie, himself, gives the answer in his cherished verse, entitled *"Confidence"*: *When shadows fall athwart thy path, 'Tis God Who Passes By! Bow down in peace and praise and pray, rind even while you sigh, Remember this Each sorrow is a shadow sweet That tells how near Christ's nailed feet Arc walking by thy side 'Then Let Thy Soul Confide!*

Yes, it was God who passed by, the God Whom Jimmie faithfully adored. Let your souls confide.

The mystery is ongoing.

A SUPER WEIGHTY EVENT

1956

"What the hell? This can't be the right one!" A red-faced trucker waved his pink slip at me from the other side of the window.

I looked at him through dazed eyes. I was eighteen, working for the coal mining company where my dad was the superintendent. It was my first day of weighing loaded coal trucks on my own. Across the yard from our small building, a tipple dropped coal into truck beds. Each truck pulled onto the scale outside the window of our weigh station.

After a three-month healing period following my near-death experience, I had been hired as assistant to the payroll clerk, Ruth Patsch, with the caveat that I would receive no special treatment from anybody, *especially* my father. The office Ruth shared with me was located up three steps and across the hall from the small weigh station where I stood. The office of our chief accountant, Mr. Bob Russell, was down the hall to the right.

Until today, Ruth and Mr. Russell had shared the disruptive job of weighing trucks. Having to halt their clerical tasks, they took turns dashing to the weigh station each time they heard the grinding engine of a truck leaving the tipple.

Both of them were greatly relieved when my weighmaster's license arrived yesterday. Soon after it came in the mail, Ruth trained me then she or Mr. Russell watched over my shoulder and gave suggestions as I weighed and wrote slips.

Now the driver was pounding on the glass, and gawking at me, "Are you even awake, for Chris-sake?" His truck idled on the scale out front.

Mr. Russell trotted down the three steps into the weight room as fast as his elderly legs could move him, "Watch your tongue, man!" he shouted. Brow furrowed, he peered at the trucker's hostile face. "So, what's your complaint?"

The trucker moaned, "I know she's new, Bob, but time's money to me! She takes forever to write a slip! So I hurry in here to spell out my name and numbers—and she hands me this!"

He waved the slip again. "It's gotta be wrong! Either she's made it up, or it's from some other trip." He slammed it down and slid the paper through the opening in the window. "There's no way she wrote it up that fast!"

I felt bad for holding the truckers up. From years of experience, both Ruth and Mr. Russell completed slips almost without pause as soon as a truck pulled onto the scale. Glancing out the window at a truck approaching head on, they recognized the driver and knew his account number, license number and empty truck weight by heart. By the time his truck was on the scale and the driver appeared at the window to get his slip, the only item left to fill in might have been the driver's destination if it wasn't a repeat. Some fleets or freelance drivers ran loads to the same contractor for days or weeks. In those cases, the same destination was repeated for each slip and could be written out before the driver appeared at the window.

I was expected to share the responsibility and eventually provide the same swift service to the drivers. But so far I'd been nothing but a drag on the operation. Even after my day of training, the men were virtual strangers to me. On this, my second day of writing slips I had nothing memorized—not even the name of one single man! I had to wait for each driver to give me his information, starting with his name and usually its spelling because many of the Eastern European names defied phonetic logic.

Mr. Russell picked up the driver's pink slip and walked over to check the numbers on the scale.

"The load weight's right," he paused and glanced at the big clock.

"The time of day is right," he continued to examine the slip.

"Your company name's right."

"Your account identification number is right..."

"The spelling of your name is even correct," he glanced at the driver and smiled, "and the license number checks out."

The driver pulled off his cap and shook his head. "Something's gotta be wrong!"

"Where are you taking this load?" Mr. Russell asked.

The driver told him.

"That's what it says here." Mr. Russell held up the slip and pointed to the name. "This isn't a repeat trip, is it?"

"No. It's my once-a-month delivery," he answered. "How could she possibly know my destination?" He looked baffled.

Mr. Russell looked at the board to confirm that the white copy and yellow copies of the given pink slip were hanging on their proper nails. They were.

"There's nothing wrong with this slip," he said, handing it back to the driver. "It's definitely your slip for this load."

The driver shook his head in bewilderment. He snatched the slip up and shrugged his shoulders.

Leaning forward he looked at me wide eyed, "How'd you do it? Not even Bob here can turn out a weigh slip *that* fast—and he has all our stuff in his head!"

He studied the slip and looked back at me. "How'd you do it?"

Mr. Russell asked gently, "Can you answer him, Emily? Do you know what you did?"

I felt headachy and befuddled. "Yesterday…at the end of work Ruth told me she wouldn't be here today…and I would be doing most of the weighing. She said I should listen for the sound of a truck pulling out from the tipple and hurry down to start the slip before the driver came to the window."

"And?" Mr. Russell asked.

"I…had a headache this morning. When I heard the truck pulling away from the tipple, I hurried down here and wrote today's date and Greensburg-Connellsville Coal and Coke Company on the top line before the truck reached the scale. I don't…remember anything after…until…I heard him screaming at me."

Out the window I noticed a truck waiting to move onto the scale and another truck's engine was grinding as it moved its load from under the tipple. *Those guys are really going to be mad,* I thought to myself. In addition to my headache I felt shaky and lightheaded. "Mr. Russell… I think I'm going to be sick," I said helplessly.

He sent me back to the office I shared with Ruth. After weighing the waiting trucks, he called my mother.

At home I rested and tried to remember writing out the slip. Nothing at all came to me. After writing the company name, I had blanked out until the driver's shouting brought me back.

This event happened in the days when most bookkeeping required heavy writing through sheets of carbon paper to produce triplicate copies. The original went to company headquarters, the yellow slip went into our office file, and the pink one went to the driver. The coal mine contracted with two or three trucking companies with small fleets and also a variety of freelance truckers.

As I mentioned, most of the men had ethnic names, the spellings of which gave no phonetic clues to their pronunciations. In addition, account numbers were long concoctions of digits and letters. The weight of the empty trucks might have matched other trucks of the same year and model, but the empty truck weights varied. A truck's license plate could be seen as the truck came across the yard but the names of the companies or freelancers who owned the trucks were located on the doors, which were not visible until the truck was on the scale. Not all trucks had names on them.

Trucks from the same company often delivered to a single destination throughout a day, a week, or even months. On my second day I couldn't distinguish among the trucking companies just by looking at a truck head on. Almost all the trucks were red regardless of their model or their company. They looked the same to me except some were older than others.

Throughout the preceding day, I had written the same destinations on numerous slips because many trucks had been hauling coal to the same places. But the destination for that load was unique. It was not a repeat destination. It was the only one for the month and wouldn't be repeated until the following month.

After word got around the drivers teased me, calling me the Weighmaster Witch.

"Where's my slip?" one would say as soon as he came to the window, "Aren't you supposed to have it for me by now? You did it once, can't you do it again—or all the time?"

I was asking myself the same questions—and more: How did it happen? Why did it happen? Will it happen again?

I have since learned that this kind of phenomenon is known as automatic writing. The briefest definition I could find on the Internet is: "Automatic writing is the process, or product, of writing material that does not come from the conscious thoughts of the writer."

It never happened again.

FIND OF A LIFETIME

1960

After beginning my job at the mine office, I started taking piano lessons. My intention was to keep myself occupied at home so I wouldn't be tempted to spend money frivolously on other diversions.

My piano teacher was a charming and fascinating single man, seven years older than I. In no time I had a mad crush on him and could think of little else other than Carl. Seeing the cow-eyed adoration written all over my face, he finally asked me out, explaining that he needed a date for an upcoming dance at his country club. Would I like to go?

Country club! Well, yes!! I could barely contain myself. Of course I would need the right dress—and then there was my dad. Would he permit his eighteen-year-old daughter to go out with an older man? I got Mom to sweet-talk him but Dad insisted that Carl come to our house and request his permission. Carl complied and gave Dad his word that he would neither tempt me nor permit me to drink alcohol in his company.

On the big night, Carl arrived in his tuxedo and I, like a princess, joined him in my fashionable cocktail dress (bought on Mom's credit and paid back in monthly installments).

Dancing the night away in a gorgeous, chandeliered ballroom with a charming man—and great dancer—literally swept me off my feet! His witty friends accepted me warmly without giving notice to my non-alcoholic drinks.

They jokingly accused Carl of "robbing the cradle" and warned me of his villainous reputation, all in great fun. Everything seemed to click. For me it was a magical evening.

Heeding my Mother's advice that I should be wary that Carl might attempt to take sexual advantage of me, I told him after the dance that I was not interested in a sexual relationship with him or anybody else. He pulled his car up beside my house and walked me to the front door. Thanking me for a lovely evening, he held my face in his hands and kissed me on the forehead. I was smitten!

That was the beginning of many similar dates. Carl was always the perfect gentleman, never making sexual advances and never inviting me to drink alcohol. As time went on, he drank enough for both of us. The more we went out to dances and parties, the more he drank. One night when it was time to leave from a party, he was so drunk that he asked his friend to drive me home.

Brokenhearted, I called Carl the following day and told him I was ending my lessons and I would not be going out with him again. What I desperately wanted was for him to tell me he would stop drinking rather than lose me. But that didn't happen. I thought my heart would never mend.

In February 1958, a year and a half after my high school graduation, I had saved enough money to enter Waynesburg College at the start of second semester. Still grieving from my breakup with Carl, I was eager to leave McKeesport and my thoughts of him behind.

Shortly after arriving on campus, I found a job in the small town as assistant to the bookkeeper for a wholesale candy company. It meant a brisk walk of almost half a mile between and after classes each day. My leisure time was almost limited to mealtime. When I wasn't in class I was at work; the rest of my time was given to studying. My busy-ness kept my longing for Carl out of mind, though not out of heart. The months flew by.

At semester's end, my employer offered me the opportunity to work full time during the summer months. My best friend Linda's parents, who lived nearby in Carmichaels, invited me to stay with them so I could continue my job and save money. I accepted.

Remaining in the Waynesburg area during the summer rather than returning to memory-filled McKeesport was an effective antidote for my heart's obsession. Meanwhile, my dad had resigned from the Hubbard Mine and accepted a job at a mine in Clearfield County. My parents' new location in north central Pennsylvania was at least four hours from Waynesburg.

At the start of my second semester, I was greeted by a wonderful surprise. The Dean of Women, Nancy Cairns, also my French instructor from the previous term, came to me with an offer of a "working scholarship." By serving as her office secretary between and after classes, I would receive fully paid room and board. What a gift!

Heaven seemed to shine on me that whole semester. First, I had more time to study because Dean Cairns' office was near my classrooms, not across town. Second, I joined a great sorority, Alpha Delta Pi, where I made friends and felt warmly accepted. Next, I was chosen by the Delta Sigma Phi fraternity to ride atop their homecoming float as their designated "queen" and fraternity sweetheart.

Ironically, my heart still yearning for Carl, I hadn't dated anybody on campus, but I loved going to the "Delt" parties and dancing with several of the guys who also loved to dance. I was surprised and honored when the fraternity chose me as their homecoming queen.

Then my dream of dreams came true! Shortly after

homecoming I received an unexpected phone call from Carl! In short, the man I hadn't seen nor spoken to since our breakup was calling to ask me to marry him! Not only that, he also offered to finance my schooling if I would transfer to a college near Pittsburgh. I was thrilled! At the same time, I felt confused and a little suspicious because I hadn't heard from him for so long. I told him I would have to take some time to consider his proposal.

Immediately afterward I called home to talk it over with Mom. I replayed the phone conversation with Carl almost word for word, unaware that Dad was also on the line. Mom advised me not to make an impulsive decision.

After my eight o'clock class the following morning, I returned to my room and found Dad there waiting for me. He had come for two reasons: first, to ask me to carefully examine the depth of my love for Carl before accepting his offer, as in would I be willing to spend the rest of my life caring for him if he were crippled in a car accident; second, would I please transfer to Indiana College in Indiana Pennsylvania, closer to their new location, if he paid for my education and all my needs. He told me that Mom had been struggling with some depression along with ovarian problems. She would likely be facing surgery in a few months.

Not only did Mom's needs take precedence, I was uncomfortable with accepting Carl's offer after I had worked so hard to get over him. By force of will, I turned him down.

In February 1959 I moved into Sutton Hall on Indiana's campus. After a few months I met and began dating Dave, a fine young man a few years older than I, who was attending college on the G.I. Bill.

In April, during my second semester at Indiana, another life-changing event occurred. Following an attack of appendicitis in the middle of the night, I ended up in surgery for an appendectomy. Eight hours later, I came out of a coma and remained in the hospital for more than two weeks.

Later the surgeon told me that as the needle containing the anesthesia broke my skin, my body convulsed violently and I lost consciousness. He said about one in a million patients were known to die from certain types of anesthesia, but he had never known a case where the patient survived. He warned me that I should never again have surgery without informing the anesthesiologist of my reaction. He also told me that he had removed my appendix after I lost consciousness.

Weak and depressed after my hospital stay, I was taken to my parents' home in Clearfield County. College finals were over and I had missed all the make-up dates, so basically I lost the entire spring semester.

I languished in a funk for weeks at my parents' home until the option for a fresh start came along. Connie, a longtime acquaintance and daughter of my parents' best friends was planning a move to California. A former military nurse, she had accepted a job of managing a private nursing home near Los Angeles. Connie had visited me in the hospital several times. Hearing of my lethargy—and I suspect being strongly encouraged by her parents—she invited me to go with her to California for a change of scenery. The plan was that we would share an apartment, I would get a job and eventually enroll in a college. The costs for education in California were lower than those in the east.

After Dave and I expressed our sad goodbyes, Connie and I struck out cross country in her new air-conditioned Ford Fairlane 500. The venture was just what I needed to rejuvenate my mind and spirit.

The journey was a wonderful delight in itself! Along

Route 66 I took mental snapshots of the Gateway Arch of St. Louis, red earth in Oklahoma, sage brush rolling across the highway near Albuquerque, and a barren stretch of desert before we veered off the road for the highlight of our drive: a dazzling overnight in Las Vegas.

We stayed at the Stardust Hotel and saw the hottest and most publicized new show from Paris, *Le Lido,* in which elegant women in gorgeous plumes and sequins strutted bare breasted across the stage. To a coalminer's daughter, who had barely traveled outside Pennsylvania, the show was a major thrill!

Just when I thought there would be no more surprises along the way, I experienced a sight I vowed to remember forever. The Sierra Nevadas emerged before us just as the melody of "Tara's Theme" from the movie, *Gone with the Wind,* began playing on the car radio. We turned up the music's volume and inhaled the majestic beauty of purple mountain peaks silhouetted against a sunset sky glowing orange pink and painted with swirls of white clouds. Ahh, to this moment I savor that memory of sacred bliss.

In California, Connie and I found an affordable apartment near Los Angeles in San Fernando Valley where Connie's Aunt Norma and Uncle Merle Bennett lived with their son and daughter, Terry and Judy, who were close to my age. The Bennetts soon became my second family.

Connie and I spent most of our evenings with the Bennetts watching television or playing cards. Terry and Judy were like my own cousins. Judy worked as a clerk on a military base. In her free time, she drove me around to acquaint me with the area. When Terry didn't have a date on a weekend he'd take me to a club or amusement park. After a few months he left for the Marines.

I found a job as assistant bookkeeper in a finance company office but didn't move forward on finding a college. Meanwhile, Judy included me in her social life as much as possible.

Before long I started dating sporadically on my own. That was my reality check. I found myself comparing the few guys I dated with Carl. Yes, I still carried the torch!

One evening in a moment of weakness, I called Carl to see if he had given up on me and married someone else.

As soon as he heard my voice, Carl exclaimed, "Where are you? I've been trying everything I know to locate you!"

At his words, my heart started beating out of my chest! I told him I was living and working in California.

"You can't stay there!" He insisted. "You belong here in Pennsylvania! Please come home and marry me!"

Carl followed up the call with flowers, more calls and letters. I made my decision and after a month or so arranged to leave my job and return home to marry him.

Meanwhile, my surrogate Aunt Norma landed in the ICU on life support after having a surgical procedure. Terry had been home on leave from his Marine base in Fort Pendleton and wanted to extend his leave to be at his mother's side. In those days before faxes and emails, the quickest way for him to deliver the doctor's verification to his commanding officer was to drive to the base.

That's how I ended up as a passenger on the freeway from Los Angeles to Fort Pendleton. My job was to help keep sleep-deprived Terry awake during the round trip.

In spite of the night's chill, we cranked down the windows, hoping the rushing air and traffic noise would help keep him alert. To talk, we shouted above the noise. We had been on the road for an uneventful hour when Terry yelled, "What's that up ahead?"

A cloud of smoke hovered over the freeway. As Terry slowed, we saw a crumpled four-door sedan in a dust cloud on the broad median to our left.

"An accident!" he shouted. "That car's been hit!"

We rolled onto the gravel. "Stay here and see what you can do. I'll find the nearest phone and call for help."

I hopped out and he sped away.

Dust and smoke swirled around the crumpled hood of the car. I paused for a moment hoping a door would open and somebody would come out. From where I stood, I couldn't see any movement inside the car. Approaching warily, I looked into the front passenger window. A woman's head was face down on the dashboard. Blood oozed and pooled from under her spread of black hair. The driver, a short, balding man, was slumped against the steering wheel, his head turned away, arms hanging limply at his sides.

Neither of them moved. I thought they both must be dead. I had never been at the scene of an accident before. I started to tremble.

What I saw in the back almost made me faint. The bloodied body of a young woman—maybe a teen—was hideously arched backward, her face buried against the seat. A chrome strip protruded from her bloody breast.

I gasped for breath and backed away from the car. My body was shaking uncontrollably. To get hold of myself I staggered backward, sucking in air with every step.

At first I think I walked in circles then slowly wandered through waist-high weeds as cars whizzed by.

The median was about seventy-five feet wide with tall wispy weeds growing up through a cover of gravel. The area was well lit by lights on high utility poles.

I continued to distance myself from the car as I rambled aimlessly through the weeds. Finally, I had a thought. Moving toward the side of the freeway facing oncoming traffic, I walked along the edge and waved my arms frantically in hope that somebody would pull over. Nobody even slowed. The wind from the speeding vehicles flailed the weeds against me as though they were urging me to *do something!*

Feeling helpless, I couldn't think of what I could possibly do. I had no training or experience. My only hope was that Terry would return soon with help. The shaking of my body was slowing to a general tremor.

Reluctantly I began circling back toward the car. To bolster my courage I stopped, took deep breaths and ran my hands over my face. When my hands slid down my cheeks, my head was bent, my eyes cast downward.

To my utter shock, a baby lay at my feet! Another step forward, I might have kicked or crushed it!

Sinking to my knees, I stared at the infant. It was in a white top and diaper. I couldn't tell if it was a girl or boy. Its eyes were closed, its little limbs splayed on the ground like a rag doll somebody had tossed away. How did it get there? Was it alive?

I thought it must have come from the car somehow, but we were at least fifty feet away. I wanted to pick it up but worried if that was the right thing to do. My mind raced trying to recall everything and anything I had ever learned about medical emergencies. I remembered that a person without medical training should not attempt to move an injured accident victim. Maybe the baby's back was broken.

From the light of the utility pole I could see no blood. The baby looked to be about three or four months old. Placing my ear to its little chest I listened for a heartbeat, but the highway noise prevented me from hearing anything.

I also knew babies' bones are rubbery, not as likely to

break. Then I considered that the little body lay on gravel rather than on solid concrete, so I gently flexed the tiny arms and legs. Nothing seemed to be broken.

Feeling numb, I took deep breaths and made the decision to pick up the limp body, not allowing myself to think about what I would do if the baby were dead.

Gently, gently, I slid my hands under the small torso and lifted the limp baby toward me. Its little head flopped onto my shoulder as I stood. Warm liquid oozed down the back and front of me.

Shakily, I turned and slowly faced in the direction of the car. What I saw caused me to freeze!

The driver, whom I thought was dead, had somehow come out of the car and was peering through the window into the back seat. Grabbing his head with both hands he started screaming and running fitfully—first one way, then another.

I panicked! Holding the baby firmly and securing the small head against my shoulder, I trotted toward the hysterical man as fast as I could make myself go.

The infant began to cough and heave convulsively. More warm liquid flowed. I knew it was blood. Then the baby started to wail. I wanted to scream along with it. Maybe I did.

The shrieking man was now heading toward the speeding cars on the highway! I nestled the squalling infant inside my arms like a football and ran with all my strength, circling in front of the delirious man like a sheep dog herding a stray. Fortunately the man, perhaps Mexican, was short and of average weight. Using my light five-foot-two frame to full advantage, I shielded the baby and rammed myself against the screaming man again and again, nudging him away from the highway.

He stumbled backward with each blow until we finally reached the car. I maneuvered him toward the front fender on the passenger side and was finally able to pin him against it. He kept howling and trying to wrench free but I jolted him back each time. His shrieks and the baby's screams rattled my senses and tore at my heart. I was desperate for somebody to stop. Nobody did. I wondered how long it would take for Terry to get help to us.

We remained there for what seemed another fifteen minutes. At last, several ambulances and police cars arrived.

Someone lifted the crying baby from my arms. Attendants surrounded the man and spoke gently to him. His shrieks subsided to a whimper. I heard him sobbing as they passed by toward an ambulance.

I started to cry and shake again. An attendant took me to the open back of an ambulance and gave me water to drink and wet cloths to clean my skin. One side of my body, front and back, was drenched with blood.

I saw that the passenger door to the damaged car was open and was surprised to see the woman sitting forward holding a towel to her face. Attendants stood by with a stretcher. I didn't see anybody remove the girl's body from the back seat.

Eventually, a policeman came over, wrote down my name and Terry's name, and questioned me about what I knew and saw. Dabbing my tears, I told him about Terry seeing the smoke over the freeway and what I'd experienced after Terry dropped me off.

"Em, are you all right?" Terry called as he sprinted toward me looking concerned. He stared at my blood-soaked clothes.

"Oh," I said, my mind elsewhere, "the blood isn't mine. It's from the baby I found."

"Baby?" Terry asked.

"You're Terrence Bennett, I assume," the policeman said, checking his notes and looking at Terry. "We'll want to ask you some questions."

"Yes sir," Terry replied in military style.

Looking back at me, the policeman asked, "So where was the baby?"

"Lying in the weeds," I answered. "How's the baby doing? Is it going to live?"

"The medics seem to think he'll be okay," he answered.

"Oh, it's a boy!" I said, realizing I hadn't known the baby's gender.

"In the weeds, where?"

"Over there," I pointed.

"He must have been thrown from the car somehow," the policeman pondered. "What drew you to him? Did you hear him crying?"

"No, I think he was unconscious. He looked dead to me."

"Where were you when you saw him?" the policeman asked.

"Standing right over him," I said.

"How's that?" he asked.

"At first I didn't know there was a baby. After seeing the people in the car, I was pretty shaken. Thinking they were all dead, I walked away and wandered through the weeds. Then I walked down the side of the road a ways trying to wave somebody down. That didn't do any good, so I headed back toward the car. I stopped to clear my head and when I looked down, the baby was at my feet."

"Are you saying you…stumbled upon him?" he asked.

"In a way, I guess. I just stopped for a second to compose myself. When I looked down, the baby was at my feet," I said. "That's how I found him."

An ambulance attendant who had joined us said, "That's one lucky baby boy!"

"How's he doing?" I asked.

"We think he'll be fine, thanks to you," he said, moving toward me. He placed a hand on my unbloodied shoulder and looked into my eyes. "You saved that baby's life, you know. He was bleeding internally from the impact. If you hadn't found him, he would've drowned on his blood."

Before I could respond, Terry said, "That's fantastic, Em!"

I was about to break into tears again when the policeman asked, "Can you show me where you found him?"

"It was over there somewhere," I pointed. Terry helped me from the ambulance and we walked with the policeman out to where I thought I had found the baby.

"There's lots of space out here," said the policeman, "and there's nothing that I can see, like a diaper bag or toys or anything on the ground or in the car, that would indicate that a baby had been one of the passengers." He turned and surveyed the area in every direction. "These tall weeds hide the ground pretty well. If you'd walked in any other direction, you probably would have missed him."

"What caused the accident?" I asked.

"My men are checking out a drunk driver on the other side. We think he entered this freeway facing traffic." He looked at Terry. "You should have seen headlights coming toward you. Didn't you see the collision?"

"No sir," Terry answered. "All I saw was smoke on the freeway and that car just as it sits there."

The policeman looked back at the damaged car. "The two cars must have hit and spun off in opposite directions."

"How's the other driver?" asked Terry.

"He crossed three lanes of traffic without hitting another car!" Shaking his head, the officer added, "He's walking away with some bruises. But these poor folks are his victims…the girl is dead."

I nodded sadly, "I thought she was."

"I figure the young mom in the backseat was holding the baby when the cars collided," said the policeman. "The back doors sprang open," he gestured with his hands, "flinging the baby out. When the car spun to a stop over there, the doors slammed shut." He brought his hands together making a clapping sound.

"Will the older man and woman be all right?" I asked.

"They'll need some work," said the policeman. "The man is banged up and traumatized. I think the woman lost her front teeth. She probably has a broken nose and maybe a concussion but they should survive all right."

"That's a good thing," said Terry. He nodded toward me and said to the policeman, "Is there anything more you need from us, Officer? We really need to get back on the road. My CO is expecting me."

Terry and I gave the policeman our personal information and left the scene. Neither of us was in danger of falling asleep on the drive to the Marine base. We talked about the accident most of the way. Terry procured his extended leave, and we returned to Los Angeles completely exhausted.

After a few days, the doctors informed the family that Norma had survived her crisis. Terry returned to duty at Fort Pendleton. I was back to my excitement and happiness about returning to Pennsylvania and marrying Carl.

The police contacted me a few times asking me to testify against the other driver. Having no evidence to give, I refused. Somebody showed me a small mention of the accident in a newspaper.

The article merely stated the time and location of the accident and that it involved a Mexican family and a single driver. It announced the death of the young mother and the survival of her baby son and parents. It also said that charges against the driver of the other car were pending.

I mourned for the injured parents and the motherless baby. At the same time, I was greatly preoccupied with working out the last days of my job and preparing to leave California. Filled with excited anticipation of marrying Carl, I was relieved to be uninvolved in the trial.

Knowing I would never see the family again I made no effort to preserve the article or remember their name. A few weeks later, I returned to Pennsylvania where I have lived ever since.

Throughout these intervening years, I've married twice, taught school, raised three children, and retired from my profession. Yet the memory of that accident remains vivid in my mind.

When I consider that the baby in the weeds could have been one of my own children or grandchildren, the reality of how hugely significant it was that I happened to be there looms large in my mind and heart.

I have pondered the whole event and realized the oddities of it. Surely Terry and I weren't the first and only people to see that there had been an accident. Other drivers could have stopped, but didn't. Of all people driving by, I wonder how many were facing a crisis as Terry was. He could easily have driven by to save time or just pulled off at the first exit to call an ambulance and continued on his way.

What compelled Terry to stop and drop me off?

What led me to the baby's precise location?

It's my deep regret that in the immaturity of youth I failed to learn the family's name. I have dreamed and thought about that baby boy. He's a man now, maybe even a grandfather. I wonder who he is.

When we try to make sense of outcomes to which no answer seems plausible, we sometimes say, "It was meant to be." I'll never know how I "happened" upon the baby in those high weeds. In my heart of hearts I feel I was guided to find him.

Maybe it really was "meant to be."

MESSAGES THROUGH ORANGE GLASS

1963

It was a cold Friday night in March 1963. I waited up for my husband, who was playing a gig at a popular piano bar. During the day, Carl was a newspaper reporter who jokingly referred to himself as "a reporter who never misses a beat." The occasional gig was an enjoyable way for him to increase income after I was no longer working.

It was after eleven. Carl usually got home near midnight. I had put our daughter to bed for the night, folded and stored the last of our laundry, and taken a shower.

Now I was sitting in the living room leafing through a *New Yorker* and half listening to the Jack Parr show. I didn't always stay home. Sometimes I'd get a sitter and go with friends to Nino's where Carl played. We'd have a late leisurely dinner and Carl would join us during breaks.

My husband was a charming man with charisma and a witty sense of humor, all of which made him a hit in any crowd. I pictured him effortlessly sliding from one melody to the next while keeping up his banter with admiring patrons sitting at the piano bar with their drinks and lit cigarettes.

Feeling bored and restless, I put the magazine aside and eyed my toddler's first pair of shoes on a nearby table where they awaited a first coat of white polish. I reached for them. Little Marion had been walking long enough to scuff the high-top shoes, her first pair of hard soles.

Tugging at the laces and pulling them through the small eyelets, I realized that polishing my baby's shoes was a "first" for me. I thought of my dear mother-in-law, Marion. She had known her first grandbaby, born to her first and only son for only three brief months before her death. Her little namesake had been her greatest happiness at life's end. She had literally willed herself to stay alive so she could know this grandchild.

I thought of how Marion and Chris had adopted Carl right after his birth when Marion was age thirty-nine. By the time Carl and I married, my mother-in-law was in her late sixties and Chris, a few years younger than she, was nearing retirement.

I smiled to myself remembering the first time I met Carl's mom.

I had been so nervous that afternoon. Never having met nor seen Carl's invalid mother, I had read some of her poetry, which the local paper carried occasionally, and heard talk of her legendary singing voice. British born and trained in classical voice, she'd soloed in professional and church choirs in the Pittsburgh area while she was still able to get around. I also knew her reputation as a well-loved healer who, years before, had nursed sick children of the very poor back to health with her poultices and natural remedies.

As we approached the front door, Carl kept assuring me I had nothing to be nervous about. We entered the house and he escorted me into the living room where his stately, white-haired mother, crippled by rheumatoid arthritis, was seated in her chair. She was wearing a tasteful mauve silk dress with pearls at her neck. A black cane rested at her side, even though she could no longer walk.

"Mother, this is my darling Emily. It's time the two of you met." Glancing from his mom to me, he added, "Knowing you both, I'm sure you'll have no problem getting acquainted. I'll be in the back." He tossed me a wink and left.

Marion's presence filled the room. She was soft and powdered, wearing wire-rimmed spectacles, one lens of which was frosted. The glasses did little to hide the attentiveness of her large intelligent eyes. Her face warmed me with kindness, causing my nervousness to dissolve.

She smiled, and in a rich British accent, she said, "Emily." Her speaking voice was surprisingly robust, yet as lilting as rippling water. Pausing as though playing back the melody of my name in her head, she repeated very slowly "Em-i-ly."

She smiled again lovingly. "Your name is like a poem."

Taking in the sight and sound of her, I remembered Carl telling me she suffered also from diabetes, glaucoma, and heart congestion. Concern and pity must have shown on my face, for she said knowingly, "Don't pity me, my dear. The Lord never gives us anything we can't handle."

Her dignified manner and grace enthralled me. That day marked the beginning of a close, loving relationship between us.

Laughter from the TV brought me back to the present. The shoes and laces were in my hands. I set the shoes aside and held up the laces for inspection. Glancing past them I noticed the baby grand piano across the room. The memory of Mother Marion's first and only visit to our apartment flowed into my mind.

She and Carl's dad, Chris, had come for dinner to celebrate my pregnancy. After the four of us had eaten, Carl and Chris carried Marion from the wheel chair to the sofa so she could lie back while Carl played some Mozart and Chopin for her.

While relaxing afterwards, she peered at the evening sun through an orange-colored wine decanter that stood on the table between her and the window. She said it reminded her of a childhood antic in England when she got a spank for running outside with two red crystal glasses wanting to look through them at the bright sky and fluffy clouds.

When she had finished her story we announced that our baby girl—or boy—would bear her name. The spelling of her name, Marion, would be appropriate for either gender, we teased.

Her large eyes opened wide and a smile brightened her face. "Oh," she said happily, "I cannot think of a greater honor!"

The dull white shoelaces lay in a loose tangle on my lap. I picked up the shoes beside me, pulled out the tongue from each and sniffed the insides where those little feet had sweated a sweet musky odor into the leather. My mind remained anchored in the past and I thought of the valiant way Mother Marion had fought to live so she could meet the precious wearer of these shoes.

My dear mother-in-law had been in the hospital with pneumonia for days with no sign of recovery. I was seven months pregnant standing at her bedside watching her pallid face through a transparent oxygen tent. Her eyes were closed. I'd been there for hours while Carl and his dad were at work. Nurses had been in and out of the room checking her vital signs. When I'd raise my eyebrows as a way of asking if there were any improvement, the response always came as a somber shake of the head.

I remember slipping my hand under the plastic tent and gently holding Marion's satin-skinned, arthritic hand.

She opened her eyes and slowly turned her white head toward me. In her British accent she whispered, "My dearest Emily. How long have you been standing?" She stopped to breathe. "Get off your feet, love, and rest." Another breath. " Don't concern yourself about me." Breath. "I will live to see our baby Marion." Short pause. "I promise you that, my darling."

A loud television commercial interrupted my reverie.

Rising from my chair, I turned off the TV and continued to the coffee table where I removed the classified pages, which we never read, from *The Daily News*. After spreading the paper on the TV tray, I went into the kitchen, doused the laces in sudsy water for soaking, then wiped the shoes with a damp cloth.

I recollected how tiny our baby Marion was at birth! She had been premature by almost four weeks. I wondered if her early birth had been luck or Providence. I would never forget the day we brought her out of the hospital.

A nurse's aide opened the glass door of the hospital's main entrance and I stepped into the cold noon air, swaddling our baby in my arms. Carl came around and helped me into the bucket seat of our Thunderbird. On the drive to his parents' home, he kept looking over at our newborn daughter and me. I'd glance back at him and smile, barely able to take my eyes from our precious infant's tiny face.

At the home of the new grandparents I gently placed our newborn into the feeble, waiting arms of her loving grandmother. Beaming with joy, Marion looked into her granddaughter's face. Carl, his dad, and I waited expectantly to hear what she would say. She said nothing. Instead, she began singing an English lullaby. I was surprised and enraptured!

The melodious voice that surged from her frail body was full-throated and resonant. Its tone was tender, passionately loving and mournful, more goodbye than lullaby. I ducked into the next room swabbing tears from my face. Carl and his dad followed. The three of us huddled together and cried.

"You know," Chris said, blowing his nose, "she was singing in the Met when first we dated."

Checking a shoe for dryness, I realized that tears had come to my eyes from reliving that sweet moment. I ran my hand over the leather then ambled back into the living room. Examining the raw grey leather of the scuffed toe, I wondered how my newbie toddler had inflicted such damage.

Dousing the toe with white polish, I returned to my reminiscence of Marion, the last time we were together.

It was in a hospital room again. I sat beside her bed watching dear Marion, eyes closed and struggling to breathe. Each of her breaths made a raspy sound. I wasn't sure if she were asleep or unconscious.

A nurse entered, fluffed Marion's pillow and left the room.

"Emily...my dear." I bolted to my feet. "Please...remove my rings."

"No...no," I pleaded. "I don't want to do..."

"Please, my darling," she insisted, taking a few labored breaths, "Pass them on to our precious baby...from me." Another rattled breath. "Remove them...please." Breath. "Do it for me...and for baby Marion."

I reluctantly did as she asked.

She closed her eyes and drifted away again. I sat looking at the rings in my hand, feeling mournful. After an hour or so, I dozed.

Marion startled me awake.

"Hettie!" she shouted. I sprang from my chair and took her hand. "Oh, Emily...Hettie is here!" she exclaimed. Hettie, short for Hennrietta, had been her older sister and best friend who'd died in England at a young age. Marion's glassy eyes were opened wide to something I couldn't see.

"Hettie," she said, nodding toward me, "this is my dear Emily...Carl's wife!" My sweet mother-in-law appeared ecstatic.

The nurse appeared in the doorway and stopped abruptly. Marion's gaze shifted to a place beyond the invisible Hettie. "Oh! Look at those sweet children." Her face softened, and she extended an arm, "How beautiful they are!" She was smiling, almost glowing, "Look at them, Emily... romping through fields of daisies! How lovely!" She coughed and gasped for breath.

The nurse disappeared and quickly returned with a hypodermic and slid the needle into Marion's arm. After a few minutes, the coughing and wheezing subsided. The nurse tenderly dabbed Marion's face with a moist cloth. Marion glanced in my direction, smiling peacefully. She squeezed my hand then closed her eyes.

Within minutes she was asleep.

Before an hour had passed, she was gone.

I held up the newly polished shoes and inspected them through teary eyes. Dearest Marion, who had endured endless days and nights of cruel disease and merciless pain, who had willed herself to survive so she could embrace her grandchild and sing her a lullaby, was denied seeing her darling namesake take first steps or speak baby words. She would never hear her granddaughter say *Gammaw* or *Nana* or *Gammy*, never knowing by which name she would be called.

I tried to imagine how thrilling it would be for Marion if she could see her little namesake now, walking and beginning to talk.

At that moment I heard a sound behind me. **Klink.**

A rush of exhilaration ran through me! Spinning around, I saw a stemless wine glass lying in two pieces atop the short bookcase where it and four other glasses surrounded a matching orange decanter. It was the same orange set Mother Marion had looked through during her visit. I felt her presence.

Getting to my feet I moved forward to look at the pieces. The glass had simply split in two, leaving smooth, straight edges. Not at all frightened, I wanted to laugh out loud! I could feel Mother Marion like a loving embrace. It was as though she had just spoken, "I'm here, Emily dear."

"Oh, my! You're here!" I think I said those words aloud. Speaking to her mentally, *I said, I'm so happy and grateful to know that you're still with us, Mother Marion! You are seeing Marion walk! And you will hear her put words together for the first time! Oh, Carl will be overjoyed when I show him this glass and give him the good news!*

Taking deep breaths, I stood and stared at the broken glass through my tears. Out of excitement my heart was beating rapidly.

What had just happened was hard to believe. But it did happen! Moments earlier, I had been on the brink of crying from sadness. Now I was giddy with joy! Turning slowly, I looked around the room, almost expecting to see Marion there.

I barely had time to process my reaction when I heard the key turn in our apartment door. Carl stepped inside and closed the door behind him. Before he could remove his coat, I dashed forward and threw my arms around him.

"I have the best news!" I exclaimed. "You aren't going to believe what I have to tell you!"

He hugged me back and gave me a quick peck on the lips. Slipping out of his coat, he said, "This ought to be good!" He hung his coat in the closet and turned to me grinning, "So. Did a leprechaun stop by to say we won the Irish sweepstakes?"

Taking him by the hand, I led him to the bookcase. "Look at this!" I said gesturing at the broken pieces. "It just fell apart!"

He gazed at the broken glass.

"This was one of our favorite wedding gifts." He picked

up the pieces and examined them. Then he looked down at me like a benevolent father.

"Emily, wine glasses don't just fall apart." Smiling, he added, "It's okay. I'm sure it was an accident."

"No, no! I didn't break it, Carl. I was sitting there," I explained, gesturing to the chair, "polishing Marion's shoes. The glass just…fell apart…on its own."

Without any thought of how my words might affect him, I exclaimed, "It's your mother's way of letting us know she's still around. She sees what's going on!"

"Wait, wait, wait," he said, moving toward the couch, "you're way over my head." He sat wearily and looked at me as though I had turned into a stranger. "You're not making any sense, Em." He patted the cushion beside him. "Please come sit with me sweetheart. Tell me what happened."

I sat facing him. "Carl, I know this is hard to believe. Just listen. I was sitting there polishing Marion's shoes and thinking about your mother. I almost started to cry thinking how sad it is that she isn't here to see Marion take her first steps and say her first words. At that very moment, I heard the glass break. It was lying there in two pieces. What's even more surprising is I felt her presence! I knew instantly it was your mom! I'm overjoyed! I thought you would be, too."

He shook his head and looked dismayed. My mind was still reeling but part of me realized how strange my explanation was sounding to him.

"Come on, honey," I pleaded, "I wouldn't make this up."

"Okay. If my mother's ghost is hanging around, why wouldn't she contact me instead of you? After all, I've known her a lot longer, wouldn't you say?" I felt he was simply trying to humor me.

"Hah! She could thump you on the head with that decanter and you wouldn't get it, honey. You're not open to such things. Your mom and I shared secrets. She told me about ways her sister Hettie communicated with her after she died. And she told me of her attempts to share those experiences with you but you would quickly change the subject."

"Look Em, glasses don't fall apart on their own!" He shook his head and ran his fingers through his hair. "If it broke as you say, the glass must have been defective to begin with. Maybe there was some sound wave like one of those things only dogs can hear that broke it."

"Maybe. But would a sound wave break just one of those glasses? Why not the others?" I thought for a moment. "Why wouldn't it break one of our fragile crystal ones? Those orange glasses are slightly thicker at the bottom and taper to a thin rim," I said, gesturing to the set.

"Okay. But why on earth would my mother break a glass to get in touch with you?" he asked. "I don't know much about ghosts, but I imagine that breaking a glass is a pretty tall order for something—or someone—who can't hold a hammer!"

I smiled. "She didn't break just any glass. She broke an orange glass!" I added emphatically.

"What's that supposed to mean?" he groaned

"Don't you remember your mom looking at the light coming through the orange glass and telling us the story of getting spanked for running outside with red crystal tumblers?"

"Not exactly," he said, as though I were asking him to recall the cover of last year's phone book.

"That doesn't matter," I said. "She broke the orange glass because she knew I'd connect it to her."

"I'm going to bed." He got up and headed for the bathroom.

I couldn't have felt worse if he'd slammed a door in my face.

Feeling alienated and somewhat disoriented, I sat waiting for my tangled emotions to distill down to something I could identify. Hurt? Yes. I felt hurt by Carl's reaction. Sad? Strangely enough, I wasn't sad. I was excited. Excited to know that Marion was with us!

Knowing that had changed my reality! I was now in a new place. Mars, maybe. I felt that I had veered far away from my husband. Lost. Would I find my way back?

An hour ago, I knew who I was and where I was going. I felt secure in my marriage. Now, I wasn't sure about anything.

Carl's refusal to believe his mom's presence was understandable, but his insinuation that I was lying about the broken glass had devastated me. I probably would have felt okay if he'd accepted what I'd said about the glass falling apart. But he didn't. Now, it felt as though he were punishing me.

After giving him enough time to fall asleep I went to bed, leaving the broken pieces where they lay. When I awoke the next morning, Carl was gone. So were the pieces of glass. So was the kitchen trash.

In the days that followed, I tried to convince Carl that I had told him the truth about the broken glass. He shut me down each time.

His final response was, "It's over! I don't care about how, or who, or what broke the stupid glass. It doesn't matter to me. Please don't bring it up ever again!"

An invisible wall stood between us. I felt that my husband was playing it safe with his undaunted disbelief while I was taking a risk by declaring my hard-to-believe reality. I felt isolated, confused, and alone. Even worse, I felt discredited and devalued by my husband. Getting through each day was a struggle.

I ruminated over Carl's reaction. Questions plagued me throughout each day: *Does he really believe I would lie to him about a broken glass? Why won't he talk with me about it? Will we ever get past this?* The answer to every question never changed: *I don't know.*

I worried about my own sanity. *Am I imagining all this? Could something like a sound wave have broken the glass? Was the timing a coincidence? Why didn't it scare me?*

Finally, the biggest questions of all were about Marion. *Is she here with me now? Does she know the trouble it's caused? Do I really believe Marion was contacting me? Yes. I could feel her love. Why would she do that? To let us know she loves us and is near.*

A few weeks passed. One afternoon while my daughter napped, I busied myself with tidying our dresser drawers. Under some odds and ends, I found a dainty coin purse Mother Marion had given me. She had received it from her Auntie Margaret.

Dangling the black, fringed antique by its short crocheted wrist strap, I walked into the living room, sat down on the couch, and unfastened the tiny catch. Half a British crown was tucked inside.

Seeing the halved coin, I remembered Marion telling me that when she first planned to leave her home in England to create a life in America, one of the first persons she told was her Auntie Margaret, with whom she was very close. Her aunt tried to discourage her from leaving, but Marion's decision was firm.

Before her departure, the little purse arrived in the mail from Auntie Margaret. Inside, Marion found the halved crown along with a note telling her to think of the severed coin as one-half her auntie's heart sent to love and protect her along her way. The note also declared that Auntie's heart would not be whole until the two of them could be united again in England.

I held the partial coin in my hand and ran my fingers over the tiny purse wondering how many times Marion must have done the same thinking about her dear aunt and her home in England.

Klink.

It happened at that moment!

Feeling a rush of joy, I sprang to my feet and dashed to the bookcase. There it was—a second orange glass lying in two pieces! Mother Marion was with me again! Incredible!

Again exhilarated, I spoke to her mentally: *Dearest Marion! Thank you for letting me know you're with me! Your presence fills me with happiness. But I need your help! Please, please do this again when Carl is here with me. He doesn't understand! He doesn't believe you're letting me know of your presence. He thinks I'm making this up! Please, please....*

I left the broken glass untouched where it lay in two pieces. When Carl came home from work, I resisted the urge to point it out, hoping he would see it and say something. He didn't.

He walked by it that evening, and again and again for several evenings, until I lost all self-control and exclaimed, "Haven't you noticed another glass has fallen apart? Do you see it there? Or do you choose to believe it's invisible?"

"None of the above," he replied, unfolding the newspaper, "I simply don't care about it, one way or another."

Discussion over. I gave him a sharp look, marched to the bookcase, removed the pieces of glass, carried them into the kitchen, and dropped them loudly into the trash. Retracing my steps, I snatched up my novel and escaped into our bedroom, hoping he would remain in the other room until I was asleep.

We trudged through day after day together in marriage but separate in our minds. Frustrated and alone, I wondered if the wall between us would ever come down. Our daughter sustained us through two difficult weeks. Her needs required us to be a team, and she made us laugh a little each day. This diversion managed to reduce some tension for me.

One evening after Marion's bedtime stories and goodnight kisses, Carl and I entered the living room at the same time. Casually picking up the newspaper he sat down on the sofa to read. He spread the pages open then looked up at me impishly.

"Care to join me?" he asked, smiling. He extended one arm, inviting me to sit beside him and share the paper as we used to do. After some reticence, I eased my way over and sat next to him, taking hold of my end of the paper. We both became engrossed in reading.

Klink.

Upon hearing that sound, I was struck by joy and sheer gratitude!

Carl's head jerked up. He glared at the broken glass on the bookcase.

"She did it!" I cried gleefully. "She's here!" In my head I was shouting, *Oh, Thank you, Mother Marion! Thank you!*

I watched Carl go pale. He rose and walked to the bookcase without taking his eyes off the broken glass.

"Okay…okay," he said nervously, looking frightened. "Okay…I believe you. This glass broke on its own somehow. That doesn't mean my mother's ghost did it." He shook his head, "No. No, I don't buy it."

I stood, feeling Marion's presence. "Oh, I do. More than ever!" I said with conviction. "When the last one broke, I asked her to please break another glass while you were with me in this room," I gestured toward the glass, "and she did!"

I took him by the hand. "Sweetheart, just be still. Can't you *feel* her here?"

"I'm not doing that! And this broken glass is no proof!" He was red faced. "It's nothing but a simple coincidence, Em. Obviously the glass in this wine set is defective. Either sound waves or air waves or something we can't hear or see caused the glasses to break, honey."

"What about the timing? Do you consider those three perfectly timed breaks nothing more than random coincidences?"

He shrugged. "How should I know?" He rubbed the back of his neck wearily. "Does it really matter?"

I shook my head slowly. At the same time I was realizing that Carl would not, perhaps could not open his perception to a reality he considered risky, strange and even frightening. I suddenly understood that I had been wrong in taking his reaction personally.

"Perhaps...not." I said with a wave of my hand signaling it wasn't an issue.

He took me in his arms. "Sweetheart, I owe you a big apology for not believing you about how the glasses broke. I'm so, so sorry I doubted you. Please try to forgive me."

He rocked me in his arms, then stepped back and looked me in the eyes with a grin on his face. "You gotta' admit, it's one of those 'you-have-to-see-it-to-believe-it' things."

"I'll grant you that," I said with a smile and a roll of the eyes. In my head I was saying to Marion, *I'm sorry. Carl can't get it. I think he might be afraid. I know he loves you. I love you, and I'm happy you're still with us. Thank you so much!*

"Can we bury the hatchet on this, Em? The only difference between us is our interpretation of this crazy gig. You say 'da mudda,'—I say, 'da nada,'" he said with a comic shrug of his shoulders.

I smiled and hugged him back. "Oh, I don't know. I think a small war could be fun. Maybe we should get in the ring and fight it out." I batted my eyelashes at him.

"Indeed!" He answered, smiling broadly.

Our hearts and minds coalesced, and our marriage was fun again. Carl knew for certain I was telling the truth about the glasses falling apart. I accepted the fact that he would never be able to know the special joy and comfort of his mother's presence in our lives. Neither the decanter nor any of the remaining glasses in that set broke after that night.

Carl was oblivious to my awareness that Marion remained with us. She stayed for years watching over her namesake, and our other two children, Stephen and Cara.

During those years, I felt Marion near every now and then, like a comforting breeze wafting by, never doubting that she was loving and protecting her grandchildren.

Seven years after the first glass broke, my dear mother-in-law visited me in a dream. She stood on a hillside holding a green blanket in her arms. Her hair was long and she appeared healthy and vigorous.

"My darling, Emily," she said softly. "You know I've been with you. My time has come to move on."

"You've taken good care of our children, Mother Marion," I said. "Thank you, thank you. Go with my love."

"Goodbye, dearest Emily."

"Goodbye, Marion. I will miss you."

I think I cried in my sleep that night.

DREAM NUMBER

1965

It was a normal day. Carl was at work and I had just finished having lunch with my little ones, Marion and Stephen. The radio played softly in the background as I moved about the kitchen. A news reporter said something about a car accident. His words brought back a strange dream from the previous night.

I was driving a nondescript car on a highway with a flat concrete divider separating opposing lanes. A speeding white sedan veered toward me, jumped the low divider and crashed head-on into my car.

Next I was walking down a long lighted corridor lined by doors with translucent glass windows. As I passed by, fuzzy figures of people appeared behind the windows of each room. I could hear them talking.

Some of the voices sounded familiar, but I felt it would be wrong to enter any of the rooms. I had just crashed my car. Maybe I was in a hospital or in some kind of limbo.

Behind each door a different activity or game seemed to be going on. When I reached the end of the corridor, people in the last room were playing a betting game.

"Place your bet!" a loud voice demanded.

"I bet 5-5-0," somebody answered.

"5-5-0," a different voice said.

Others repeated, "5-5-0."

When the news reporter triggered my dream, the number 5-5-0 rang in my head. I thought of how my grandfather had used a "dream book" to help him pick good numbers for gambling. He'd always ask me to tell him about my dreams so he could consult his book for guidance.

Before state lotteries were in place people took illegal chances playing the "daily number," which was somehow derived from the stock market. My grandfather and most of my uncles played the numbers all the time. Growing up, I often heard them talk about their numbers.

Chris, my father-in-law, was a bookie and player as well. In those days, playing numbers seemed like a normal thing to do for everybody but me. I had never played one in my life.

Carl wasn't much of a numbers player either, but most of the folks at the newspaper where he worked placed daily bets with John, the resident bookie.

Deciding the time had come for me to finally play, I called Carl at the newspaper. When I told him what I wanted, he reacted with surprise.

"You what?" He laughed, then shouted, "John, Em wants to play a number!"

I could hear howls and rants from our friends on the staff.

"What is it?" he asked in the muffled tone of a mob gangster, "I'll slip it to Johnny da' Book."

"It's 5-5-0," I said in a hushed tone going along with the fun.

"How'd ja come up wid dis numbah?" he asked.

"It came to me in a dream," I whispered into the phone.

"Hey John, it's 5-5-0!" he shouted. I could hear loud boos and the sound of John's voice.

"Johnny says dat's not a good numbah," Carl shouted into the phone.

"Well, it's da only numbah I got!" I said in fun. "Tell him to play it for me."

"She wants to play it anyway!" Carl shouted. "She says it's hot!"

More laughter in the background.

"How much do you want on it?" he asked.

"One dollah."

"Uh-huh. Would you like dat straight or boxed?" he asked in his bookie imitation.

"Straight," I answered. After a few more quips, we ended the call.

The number kept repeating in my mind. My intuition urged me to go for it. Next I called my father-in-law and asked him to put a dollar on it. He was amused that I wanted to bet and said he would place it.

Later that afternoon I answered my phone and heard these words:

"Emmie, this is your Uncle Johnny. Sweetie, if you ever dream another number, you must call Uncle Johnny right away. Your number hit straight up today!"

I thought, What a sweet win—one thousand dollars in cash!

I was wrong.

Sadly, I soon discovered that my take would be only half that amount. Intending to give the rookie a greater chance for winning, both Carl and his dad played my dollar to bet fifty cents for a straight hit and fifty cents for a boxed hit. In the end, my dream brought me five hundred dollars, an amount close to the number I had dreamed.

I've never dreamed another number since. (Wouldn't turn it down!)

CLEAR VISION OF A PAST LIFE

1967

Back in 1946 after Mom returned and we were living next door to Aunt Em, I would lie awake at night marveling over the way God had answered my prayers and brought our family together again.

I thought about God a lot. My thinking led me to ponder big questions: *Who am I? Why am I here? What happens when we die?*

One night during this inquisitive state, a strange awareness emerged: my name had not always been Emily! I had been known by another name before this— this life. I had an intuitive revelation that I was an ongoing soul reborn as a girl named "Emily." Whoever I had been or whatever my name had been in a previous life was beyond my ability to remember. But I *knew* I had lived before.

After breakfast the next morning, I asked my mother if she knew what happened after we died. She was standing at the kitchen sink with her back toward me. I heard a loud sigh, which sounded to me like, "Oh, not another one of Emily Ann's troublesome questions!" (I wasn't the easiest kid to have around.)

Her answers were vague. "I guess nobody knows for sure. Some people think we go to heaven, some think we go to hell if we've led bad lives."

"Does anybody believe we return to Earth in a different body?" I asked.

After a long pause she answered, "I don't know anybody

who thinks like that." Then she added, "There are some religions on the other side of the world that might hold such beliefs, but Christian churches in this country teach about heaven and hell."

Unconcerned, I declared, "I think I lived in a different body before I was born as Emily."

"Really?" she asked. "How about drying these dishes for me. Then make your bed, will you?"

Mom's disinterest told me that my "revelation" ranked next to "I saw a unicorn in my bedroom." She wasn't explicit but I got the message that such ideas "in this country" were considered wrongful thinking. But that didn't change what I *knew* to be true.

Determined to find out more on my own, I became a spiritual seeker. Not in the sense that I wandered far and wide to gather wisdom from sages. It was more like I quizzed my friends, neighbors, and relatives asking, "Have you ever thought that after we die we come back in another body as somebody else?"

From my friends I got shrugs, "I dunno's," or something like, "Jesus died and went to heaven, so that's what happens to us when we die." From adults I usually got a little laugh, a roll of the eyes, sometimes a reference to what the Bible says, but mostly "I don't know. I haven't thought about it much."

I was perplexed by the fact that nobody seemed to care!

My conviction remained with me even though, at that age, I was terrified of anything having to do with death.

Later in my teens, I attended a Methodist church and listened intently to sermons, especially during the Easter season. During that church-going period, I also read books about other religions. That's when I encountered the word "reincarnation." I reveled in the fact that countless millions of people also believed as I did and had done so for thousands and thousands of years!

After our minister and his wife hired me to babysit their two young boys, I felt free to ask Reverend Brown questions about faith and Christianity.

During one of our conversations, I asked him why Christians didn't believe in reincarnation even though it was a common belief when Christ walked the earth. He told me that early Christians for the first three or four hundred years did believe in reincarnation. He also pointed out different passages in the New Testament that allude to the belief. He explained that when church leaders were ordered by Constantine to formulate a Creed for unifying Christianity, they determined that reincarnation interfered with the Christian concept of redemption. That led to the official removal of reincarnation from Christian theology.

Aligning myself with the early Christians, I felt a little less guilty for worshiping in a Christian church while holding to my personal belief in reincarnation.

Although I felt I had lived previous lives, I didn't dwell on who I might have been before I became "Emily." It was enough for me that I had intuited on my own that I had been reborn and then learned that people all over the world also held my belief. I certainly never entertained the possibility that I would *see* myself in a past life.

But, much to my wonderment, I did!

It happened in 1967 when I was living in McKeesport with my husband Carl and our three children: Marion, five; Stephen two; and Cara, one. Our house sat high on a country ridge overlooking a forest. The windows at the back of the house looked out over the trees at the open sky to the east.

I awoke as usual one night and walked barefooted down the hall to the bathroom. On the way back I made my routine stops to peek in on my sleeping children. Returning to our bedroom I listened to my husband's slow, deep breaths, almost snores. Instead of lying down to sleep I propped my pillow behind me and sat for a serene moment to take in the pre-dawn sky beginning to lighten at the rim of the horizon. ZAP! Just that quickly, I found myself in another place and time!

The place was Siam before it was known as Thailand. I was no longer in the body of "Emily." I was spirit, all mind and awareness, completely unafraid and keenly alert, with the freedom to float unseen.

I approached an old, sprawling country palace located in a minor province of Siam and floated into a small room on an upper floor. Inside the dim room stood a tall dark-skinned girl, whom I instantly recognized as me. Wrapped in an indigo blue sarong, shoulders bare, arms long and thin, she stood still as a statue, her eyes, unfocused and staring into space. Her shiny black hair was knotted at the top of her head.

Hovering very close to her face I looked deeply into her large, dark eyes and instantly became one with her, feeling her deep sadness and depression. It was like looking into a mirror. I could both observe her and *be* her simultaneously. She was completely unaware of my presence but I knew her history.

I knew that she/I had been born one of many daughters of the noble official who governed the rural province, and she lived there in the palatial structure surrounded by an expansive courtyard and many small farming villages. The old palace, constructed mainly of wood, housed many families including those of staff, servants, tutors, and courtiers.

Her mother was one of the ruler's several unexceptional wives who had the misfortune of birthing a single daughter rather than a son. The ruler's sons were in his company almost daily, and their mothers were granted special favors. The ruler knew his sons by name, and most of them enjoyed his attention and affection. On the other hand, his daughters barely received his notice, especially those considered low in the family hierarchy.

Struggling to elevate her position among the wives and their offspring, the mother devoted her days to conniving and competing with rivals and playing up to those she deemed politically useful. She regarded her daughter as her pawn for gaining upward mobility.

The many daughters living in the palace were perpetually trained to enact traditional dances for special events and court ceremonies. Leading roles were given exclusively to the ruler's offspring. Prior to each performance, his daughters competed for those leads.

The girl's height, beauty, and grace of movement bestowed her with outstanding elegance among the other dancers; however, her lack of precision in executing the distinctive forms and positions required of wrists, hands and fingers diminished her eligibility for leading roles. Her sisters bested her in that aspect of the competition and were consistently awarded the coveted leads. The intricate positions and movements demanded intense, painful stretches of the wrists, hands and fingers along with daily practice, both of which the girl detested and avoided as much as she could.

The mother blamed the girl's lack of motivation on simple laziness and punished her by removing privileges and confining her to her room for days. She also added two private sessions of supervised practice to the daughter's daily routine. Those sessions, carried out in the room where the girl now stood, were her only activities outside her bedroom.

Confinement was not much of a punishment for her.

The half-sisters with whom she had played as a child were no longer her friends. Friendship could not last without trust; trust did not thrive in their competitive environment. The girl was accustomed to being alone most of the time. The worst punishment for her was the increased training the mother had forced on her.

In that moment she was dreading the arrival of the stern, elderly hand trainer who would soon enter the room, as usual, carrying her dreaded stick for tapping derelict fingers. The distraught girl knew the routine all too well. The unpleasant woman would be wearing her usual scowl, knowing that her apathetic student had not done the warm-up stretches and also knowing that the mother's complaints and admonishments would be hers to bear when the girl, once again, would be overlooked for a lead.

I felt the girl's misery and her loathing of the tedious and painful sessions. I also felt her resentment of being hostage to her mother's ambitions. She and I as one were deeply unhappy.

I floated to her side and took in the plain rectangular room. Three shuttered windows lined the long wall looking out into the courtyard. The windows held no glass. The shutters, which opened outward, held stationary wooden slats angled toward the ground. On the opposing long wall, a grass mat in colors of orange, brown, and gold hung above a brownish futon holding a few loose pillows. Beyond the futon a small table filled the corner adjoining the short wall in which a wooden door was centered. In the corner to the right of the door and beneath one of the closed shutters sat a straight cushioned chair and another small table. A faded mat was centered on the floor's hard wooden planks. The colors in the room, except for those on the wall, were various wood tones accented by gold threads in the pillows.

Shouts and laughter from the courtyard drew me back to the girl. She pushed open a shutter and looked out on the bright day to see four teens and a two-wheeled cart piled high with long-stemmed grains. One of the boys at the front of the moving cart held the reins of an ox; the other lay atop the grain pile shouting back at the two girls who trailed behind on foot. The girls giggled and shouted teases while tossing small stones at the smiling boy perched atop the swaying heap of grains.

The sorrowful girl watched the happy group, yearning to be one of them, longing to join in their camaraderie, to have their friendship, to experience a life free from numbing routine and loneliness. She and I in unison felt intolerable despair and deepening sadness. The door to the room began to open. ZAP!

In that moment I was in my "Emily" body! I sat wide awake, still feeling the despondency of my former self while looking at a thin rim of sunlight glowing at the edge of the horizon. The lingering anguish of my former life began to fade like the dissipating sound of an echo. My astonishment was almost uncontainable!

Trying to get a grasp on what had just happened, I hopped out of bed and stared at my husband, still asleep. Had I been dreaming? Absolutely not!

I clutched my pillow to my chest in an effort to ground myself in that dizzying moment. I had an impulse to waken Carl and tell him what I had just experienced.

I thought about what to say: "I was sitting here awake, when all of a sudden I was in Siam both observing and being in the mind of myself in a former life." Ha!

The notion of telling him about my experience was sobering. Carl had previously emphasized his disinterest in topics the least bit mystical. He certainly would not have been receptive to hearing my story before going to work that morning—or at any time! I was on my own.

All through that day, trying to "normalize" my mind through daily tasks with my children and household, I couldn't stop replaying the event in my head. I wondered what became of the distressed "me" in Siam. Did that "me" ever find love and friendship?

Then the usual questions arose: *How did it happen? Why did it happen? What does it mean?*

I asked myself if the experience held any meaning or purpose for me. The answer was and still is yes. Seeing myself in that former life revealed a new aspect of me, thereby deepening my understanding of who I am—not who Emily Rodavich is, but who *I* am.

Subsequently, more questions came up. The most curious one was about names and places. Although I was *one* with the girl, why didn't I think of her name or the name of her parents or the province her father governed?

Those questions persisted. As my awareness evolved, I acquired a few insights that apply.

My past life visit placed me inside the time frame and cultural setting of Siam and also immersed me into the life experience and emotional disposition of my former self. Those were the essential details needed to encapsulate who I was and what my life was about.

I asked myself if the names of persons and places would have improved my insight or increased the benefit of the experience.

To those ends, names were nonessential. Had I emerged from that mystical interlude with names, I would have been compelled to research Siamese historical records for weeks, months or even years, wanting to track down the family and that particular girl. Focusing my time and attention to that effort would have been like concentrating on the spelling of a person's name instead of getting to know the person.

In addition to wondering about names, I also asked myself if the soul carries over characteristics from one incarnation to a subsequent one or ones. Looking back, I recognize two details from my Siamese life that might hold influence in my current existence. They are the girl's recalcitrant hands and the color indigo blue.

In this life, my hands have been a primary source of discomfort and embarrassment. When I was in elementary school my fingers began to swell, blister, and itch from various allergies. Immunization shots helped, but nothing eliminated the problem. Even as I type this, a spot on the side of my left hand is healing from a recent bout.

Likewise, indigo blue, the color of the girl's sarong, has held a special place in this life. First, it was the signature color worn by my beloved mother, Veronica, the color in which she was buried in the year 2007. Second, indigo blue played a significant role during one of my mystical interludes described later in this book.

What I have laid out expresses my intuitive understanding of this past-life visit in an effort to relate the whole effect of it. Nobody has interpreted this event for me; nor do I wish for an outside reading. My direct insight resonates deeply within me. An outside analysis would do little to alter my innate cognition.

Could the allergic condition which sometimes limits the use of my hands in this life be linked to my disdain of hand exercises in my past life? Could the significance of the color indigo blue in this life be linked to the indigo blue of the girl's sarong?

Are these mere coincidences? I have my doubts.

YOU HAVE SOMETHING TO TELL ME

1989

After stuffing my carry-on bag into the overhead compartment, then jostling with my large tote, I slid into the window seat of the plane about to leave Sarasota for Pittsburgh with a stopover in Charlotte. I had enjoyed a week-long visit with my widowed mom, and now the flight's hours would be mine for self-indulgence. No phone calls, no students, no husband or family could interrupt me. I planned to immerse myself in reading *The Tibetan Book of the Dead,* a fascinating volume that required my full and undivided attention.

As a believer in reincarnation who had lived through a near-death experience, I was interested in learning about various religious and cultural beliefs regarding death and the afterlife. This book had more than captured my interest.

"You can use this seat for your things." A smiling flight attendant said, tapping the vacant aisle seat beside mine.

"Really?" I was delighted.

"It's the only seat on the plane that wasn't booked. Just strap everything in and enjoy." She continued moving down the aisle and checking lids of overhead compartments.

Happily, I dropped my bag onto the empty seat and fished out my book. After fastening both seat belts, I opened it and started reading where I had previously left off.

I had barely read a page before I heard a voice say, "Excuse me, please."

Glancing up I saw a trim, executive-type woman in a light gray pants suit. Unsmiling, she gestured to my ready-for-takeoff bag. "This seat has been assigned to me."

"I beg your pardon," I replied. Trying to mask my disappointment, I grappled with my bag and shoved it underneath the seat in front. "I was told this seat would remain empty."

"No doubt. I managed to get on at the very last minute." She sat, tucked her purse under the seat, and strapped in.

Her straight blonde hair hung in a swingy style I've always envied. It was parted on the side, framing a high forehead, sleek nose, and well-defined jawline. It was the kind of hair that looked as though it never got tangled or needed a comb. The woman appeared to be in her early forties. Her overly serious face was the only unattractive thing about her. I wondered how she looked when she laughed.

The plane eased out of its slot and the purring engine became louder. Angling myself toward the window, I reopened my book wanting my body language to convey my disinterest in conversation, even though the woman's demeanor indicated she wasn't interested either.

She leaned her head back as if to nap.

I was barely aware when the plane taxied down the runway, took off, and leveled after climbing to cruising altitude. Some time later the flight attendant asked, "What would you like to drink?"

"Water, please." I answered.

Before I could resume reading, the blonde woman touched my arm. "I think you have something to tell me," she said. Her face was serious.

Surprised, I responded, "I beg your pardon?"

I was smiling. She wasn't smiling back.

"I think you have something to tell me about death," she answered.

"Death?" I asked with raised eyebrows. I couldn't begin to guess what she was about.

Leaning forward, she lowered her voice, "I think things happen for a reason." After a pause she added, "I don't believe in coincidences."

"Oh?" I answered, curious about where this could possibly be going.

"I'm returning home from my father's funeral, consumed with thoughts of his death, and…the word 'death' appears at the top of every page you turn." She glared at me as though I should get her full meaning. "I feel you have something to tell me about…my father's death."

I wanted to laugh. The notion that I had anything to tell her struck me as funny, but a flash of realization told me the expression on her face, which I had taken for a scowl, was grief.

Feeling compassion, I asked, "What happened to your father? How did he die?"

Her chin trembled and her eyes filled with tears. Taking out a tissue she dabbed her face. Speaking slowly and softly, she began. "My father was a highly intelligent and accomplished man. If I said his name, you might recognize it."

I was tempted to ask but didn't. She told me he'd been stricken with a form of Lou Gehrig's disease. As his paralysis spread he went from communicating with pen and paper, to a special computerized keyboard, and finally to blinking his eyes.

"He had a wonderful mind and a great sense of humor," she went on. "Both seemed unaffected by the disease. He read books on his computer, listened to the news, and joked with people around him until he could no longer express his thoughts outside of blinking. Even then he seemed to be fully engaged and aware."

"That's so admirable," I commented. "Most of us would give up long before talking by blinking."

She nodded in agreement. "He was in a nursing facility. I used to visit him every other week, but my career has been requiring more and more of me," she wiped more tears. "It's been more than a month since I've been back...I wasn't there for him."

She covered her nose with the tissue and sobbed a little.

Not knowing what to say, I patted the sleeve of her arm to comfort her.

"I was an only child," she continued. "My mother was loving, and we were close...but my father was my best friend and confessor. Anytime I was troubled about something— nothing was off limits—Dad and I would go for long walks." She cried briefly and blew her nose. "I would unburden myself, word by word, while he listened without interrupting or judging me. By the end of our walks, I always felt better." She paused, seeming to relive a special moment.

"He was always there for me," she mumbled.

I reached into my bag and handed her fresh tissue.

Taking it, she blew her nose and sat up straight. "But...I wasn't there for him." She shook her head slowly. "The staff told me a nurse was with him when he died...but I'll never really know if he died alone, or not...I wasn't there for him." More tears.

Much to my surprise, I heard words coming out of my mouth.

"Yes. I do have something to tell you about your father's death." It was as though somebody else had spoken. I had no clue about what to say, yet I continued with a confidence that came from I don't know where!

"Your father *chose* to die alone. He was ready. Your presence would have made his passing difficult, even painful. Unable to speak, he couldn't say 'Goodbye' or 'I love you.' He didn't want his last physical sight of your face to have a furrowed brow and sad eyes. He left this earth with his favorite image of you—happy and smiling. He doesn't want you to fret over his passing!"

With absolute certainty I continued, "Know that his death was easy and peaceful. He is now FREE!" I patted her hand, "Be light of heart!"

And then I was done.

Without looking at me, she closed her eyes. The scowl was gone. Leaning her head back as if to nap she smiled softly with closed lips. Her face had a warm loveliness about it.

I sat nonplussed. My mind was swirling. Something had transpired, but I didn't know quite what it was.

She didn't open her eyes, so after a moment I pulled myself together and returned to my book. Neither of us spoke another word during the flight.

When the plane landed in Charlotte, my mind was entrenched in Tibet. I hadn't given another thought to the conversation or the woman. After leaving the plane, my thoughts were focused on getting to the nearest restroom.

As I hurried along, I heard rapid footsteps behind me. The blonde woman grasped my arm. I turned and looked into her smiling face. She was beaming! I was struck by the depth and intelligence of her large, grey-blue eyes.

"A car's waiting for me," she said, "but I didn't want to lose you before thanking you for your blessing."

"My blessing?" I asked confused.

Smiling, she answered, "I told you, there are no coincidences. You've surely confirmed my belief!"

"How's that?" I asked curiously.

"When you described my father's passing, your last words were *be light of heart*." She said the four words slowly, emphasizing each one.

"Those are <u>his</u> words!" she exclaimed, smiling brightly.

Slack-jawed I stepped back immediately, recalling how clueless I'd felt when I'd opened my mouth to speak.

"I told you about our walks when I would spill my heart out to him and he always gave me words of encouragement. What I didn't tell you was that our walks *always* ended in the same way. My father would hold my face in his hands, look into my eyes and say those words, 'Be light of heart.'" Again, she pronounced each word slowly.

"Oh my!" I whispered, not knowing what to make of it.

She squeezed my arm and looked deep into my eyes. "When you said those words, I knew your message was *real*."

"I don't know what to say...," I uttered.

She continued, "Again, thank you for your blessing. I boarded the plane with a heavy heart. Thanks to you, it feels much lighter, now." She stepped forward and hugged me.

I felt a little unsteady as we parted.

Later I reviewed hearing myself say I had something to tell her. Why did I say that? Did the words I spoke about her father's death come from my mind?

Some of them could have, especially the part about her dad's inability to say "goodbye," or "I love you." I'd probably feel that way in her dad's place. But did he really "choose" to die? Did he really want to die *alone*?

Ironically, when the flight attendant had interrupted me, I was reading about the importance most Tibetan Buddhists place on *not* dying alone. At the time of death they select a Rinpoche, meaning enlightened teacher, to help them enter an elevated spiritual plane.

Was it a coincidence that I was reading about death when the woman insisted I had something to tell her?

If the words didn't come from my mind, where'd they come from? I had said, "be light of heart," which was not in my personal vernacular. Where'd that come from?

The woman said to me, "Thank you for your blessing," and she was smiling when she said it.

The words I had spoken on the plane obviously made a big difference in the way she was feeling when we landed in Charlotte. I was thrilled about that!

Although I'll probably never know for sure what happened, I decided it *was* a blessing—for both of us.

With deep gratitude, I said in prayer, *Thank You for Your Blessing.*

AUNT EM'S DEATH

1990

If someone had asked Aunt Em as a child what she wanted to do when she grew up, I doubt she would have said she wanted to run her own business. After all, she didn't stay in school much past the third grade. Even if she could have chosen a career, girls in her day became secretaries, nurses, or teachers, not business owners.

In 1951, Aunt Emily was forty-five, childless, and in need of something more than daily housekeeping to fill her days. Uncle Raddy, who had a heart the size of Gibraltar, started a business in his storefront rental space beneath their second floor apartment and handed Aunt Em the keys. My dear aunt became the proud proprietor of "Emily's Gift Shop"!

I don't think she enjoyed anything better than standing behind the counter in her own store. When a customer asked for something she didn't have, Aunt Em ordered it right away. Before long, she stocked a hodgepodge of items from candy to crocheting thread to screw drivers.

Eventually Uncle Raddy changed the store's name from "Emily's Gift Shop" to "Emily's Variety Store." My aunt's child-like laughter, good humor and eagerness to please customers gained her popularity. Folks traveled from surrounding towns to browse or buy.

In 1973, our beloved Uncle Raddy died. Afterwards Emily's sisters took turns staying with her, concerned she couldn't manage without Raddy's help and guidance. Fortunately, her work in the variety store sustained her as she adapted to single living. Support from her customers and kind gestures from the community bolstered her. In time, she was able to go it alone.

The way she moved forward surprised everybody! First, Aunt Em signed up for driver's training. After failing the test four times, she finally succeeded and got her license. (Dad teased that the driver's license had been awarded to her for perfect attendance.)

Driving gave my aunt more than wheels; it gave her wings! She became a free and independent woman.

Emily, whose only sports in life had been smoking and crocheting, joined a bowling league. I still smile picturing her plump body—shaped more like Sponge Bob Square Pants than Barbie—in a cotton housedress and bowling shoes. One of the people who bowled in her league described Aunt Em's technique to me:

> She picks up the ball, and sort of waddles to the lane. Then she stops dead and swings her arm back slowly. As her arm sways forward, she releases the ball. It drops with a loud thud and does a slow roll toward the pins. All finished, Emily turns around with a big smile on her face and waddles back to the ball rack! (Big laugh) It's the darndest thing! Without ever looking back, she usually gets a strike or spare! She's one of our high scorers!

That's how Aunt Em became one of the town's most popular characters.

Her life improved even more a few years later when she fell for Joe. He was a tall, balding, skeletal man with wire-framed glasses. Joe was kind and helpful to her, both at home and in the store. He became her adoring companion and they lived together happily in her second floor apartment. Seeing them side-by-side at family gatherings made me think of a jovial Jack Sprat and his wife.

In early June of 1990, Aunt Em surprised me with a phone call. For twenty years our contact had been limited to seeing each other at family reunions, weddings and funerals.

"Honey, I have a tumor in my colon and I need an operation to take it out. In a few days, I'm having surgery at Mercy Hospital in Pittsburgh. Would you come and be with me before they take me into the operating room? Could you do that?"

"Of course, Aunt Em," I said. "I'm sorry you need surgery, but I'll be there for sure. Just let me know when." After a little more conversation, we ended the call. She would be eighty-four in July. I was deeply moved that she had reached out to me.

The following evening, Joe phoned and said surgery was scheduled for seven the following morning.

My husband, Ron, and I were living in a small town where I taught high school English. It was located about an hour from Pittsburgh. After contacting a colleague to cover my homeroom in the morning, I phoned Donna, my widowed sister-in-law, and arranged to spend the night at her house, located only fifteen minutes from the hospital. I packed an overnight bag and headed out. Little did I know where that journey would take me.

The sky was clear and dark, the evening cool as I drove down I-79. The radio was playing some of my favorite oldies from the seventies. Suddenly the aroma of cherry tobacco smoke filled the car. The windows were closed and there was no appearance of smoke in the air.

Thinking the scent was coming from outside, I rolled down my window and leaned my head out. Oddly, the air was clear. The aroma remained strong inside, so I opened the passenger window as well. The open windows didn't dilute the aroma in the car at all!

I raised and lowered the windows several times, progressively lengthening the open period each time with the same results. Then I gave up and closed the windows to stay warm.

The aroma was strangely familiar...it came from somebody's pipe...it was pleasant...and comforting. Then I knew. It was from Uncle Raddy's pipe!

Tears came to my eyes. I turned off the radio and felt his loving presence. *He's here with me*, I thought. I felt his loving protectiveness, the way I felt with him when I was a child.

I spoke to him mentally. Uncle Raddy, *thanks for being here! I can feel your presence and your love. Is there something you want me to know?*

In a moment, I *knew* Aunt Em would not leave the hospital alive, but I wasn't surprised or saddened. The scent of cherry tobacco and the feeling of Uncle Raddy's closeness was reassuring. I knew her time had come and she would be moving into the Light. He would be there for her.

As I neared Donna's, Uncle Raddy's presence diminished and the scent dissipated. His message to me remained in my mind.

Once inside her house, I told Donna about my experience. "I want this to go on record, Donna. What I described is exactly what happened. Uncle Raddy came to me as I drove here, and I *know* Aunt Em will die in Mercy Hospital."

"Big whoop!" said Donna, smiling. "You received a message that your eighty-four year old aunt who's having serious surgery is going to die in the hospital. Now who would ever bet against such a prediction?"

"Of course, you're right," I agreed. "I just want to establish what I experienced on my way here. I'm not trying to prove anything. There's nothing to prove. The point is that Uncle Raddy made his presence known to me and gave me the 'heads up.'" At the time, I had no knowledge of the term *clairolfaction*. I have since learned that it means the paranormal experience of a person perceiving a smell or scent that is not present in the physical world.

"Do you mind if I go to the hospital with you?" she asked. "It'll be interesting to see this through."

The next morning, Donna and I met Joe in a hospital waiting room. We chatted until a nurse came out and told us we had about a half hour to spend with Aunt Em. Knowing I needed to report to work, Joe urged Donna and me to visit first. We were led into a holding area where my aunt lay on a gurney, a white cap covering her hair. She saw us and her face brightened into a smile.

"Honey, you came! I'm so glad!" After our greetings and well wishes, Donna returned to the waiting room. Aunt Em took my hand and thanked me again for coming.

"I'm glad you called me," I said. "We haven't seen each other for a long time." I gave her hand a squeeze. "I'm happy to be here with you."

"After the doctor told me I needed surgery, Joe asked me if I wanted him to call anybody. For some reason, I thought of you, honey. I called your mom in Florida and got your phone number." She took my hand and held it in hers. "I'm sorry you had to get up so early this morning. You have to go to work today, don't you."

"Not a problem at all," I said. "How are you doing? Are you frightened to have the operation?"

"I want them to get rid of the tumor!" she said. "No, I'm not scared. These doctors, they know what they're doing."

"Are you sure you're not just having a baby?" I teased.

She gave a belly laugh, and I laughed with her. "You always did know how to make me laugh, honey," she said. "I like to remember all the fun we had together before your family moved from Carmichaels. Remember how we played jacks on my kitchen table…and your friend Linda would come over and we'd have contests to see who could go the highest?"

"I sure do. My favorite was playing canasta with you and Aunt Dolores and Aunt Ann. I was always sad when we had to end the game before it was over. I could have played all day and night!"

Her eyes shined brightly. "Me too," she admitted, "I never had so much fun before…until Joe. He makes me laugh all the time…but that's a different kind of fun from what we had when you were little."

"I'll never forget, either," I said, reaching down to kiss her on the cheek. "You do well in surgery. You'll be in my prayers today even though I'll be at work."

She reached up, pulled my face to her, and kissed me on the cheek. "Thank you for coming this morning," she said, "I love you."

"I love you too, Aunt Em," I said. "I'll leave now and give Joe a chance to make you laugh some more. I'll be back to visit in a few days."

When I got home from work, I listened to Joe's telephone message. The surgery went well and Aunt Em was in a regular room. I called Donna and we decided to go back again on Saturday, two days away.

When Donna and I signed in at the nurses station, the nurse exclaimed, "Oh, she's your relative? She's absolutely amazing—our star patient! You'd never know she's eighty-four years old!"

We heard Aunt Em's laughter from across the hall.

"Hear that?" the nurse asked, gesturing toward the room, "that's her, right there! Her sisters are visiting. She laughs all the time—even with that big incision! And—this is hard to believe—last night, she told us to take away the morphine drip! She said she doesn't need it! That's pretty unbelievable. All her vital signs are strong and she doesn't show any sign of pain. We rarely get patients like her, certainly not at her age."

Donna grinned and nudged me. "Uncle Raddy must have lied to you," she teased.

My visiting aunts, Mildred, Libby and Dorothy, greeted us with hugs. Aunt Emily looked as healthy as I had ever seen her. She was smiling as usual and told us she felt fine. The aunts took Donna and me into their sisterhood, telling funny stories not meant for ears outside the room. Our visit was upbeat and thoroughly fun.

On the way home, Donna and I couldn't stop talking about Aunt Em's remarkable resilience. I was both happy and perplexed when I thought about my uncle's presence and his message. *What was that all about?* I wondered.

A day or two later Joe called with distressing news. He had arrived at the hospital to discover that Emily was in the intensive care unit. With no sign or warning, she had suddenly lapsed into a coma. The nurses said her doctors had no explanation for the coma and couldn't predict if she would come out of it. Nobody was able to answer Joe's questions. He had stayed by her side in the ICU until the nurses asked him to leave.

I went in the following day. What I saw sickened me. Aunt Em, still as death, had intravenous tubes attached to both hands. Another tube had been inserted into one of her nostrils. Her face was puffy and featureless. Through thin strips of sheer tape, meant to hold her eyes closed, I could see the whites of eyeballs and rims of blue irises. She looked like a scary wax figure.

On my way out, I plied the nurses with questions but they just shook their heads and said they had no explanation for the coma. On the way home, I stopped at Donna's and reported what I had seen. Both of us were morose. Uncle Raddy didn't enter our conversation.

Various family members visited and questioned Aunt Em's doctors, but they were confounded. The surgery was successful. She had been recovering better than expected. Her vital signs and her appetite were excellent. She had been walking in the halls. One of the doctors had even signed her discharge papers prior to the onset of the coma. There was no indication of stroke, heart attack, aneurism, or infection.

About four days after my visit, Aunt Em came to me in the middle of the night.

Almost everybody has dreams and nightmares; and many of us experience lucid dreams. A visitation is none of those. A visitation is similar to having somebody wake you up from a deep sleep to tell you something, such as "I left your keys in the drawer," or "It's two o'clock and I just got in." You receive the message then go back to sleep. Upon arising, you remember being awakened and also what was said to you. You might even have been be in the middle of a dream when you were aroused, but you still remember the event. It was like that with Aunt Em's visit.

I was sleeping next to my husband when I was awakened. Opening my eyes, I looked up at a pretty fair-skinned woman hovering in front of me. Her hair was long and golden, her eyes, large and blue. She was in a white dress and she appeared radiant with light.

"Emily Ann," she whispered.

"Yes?" I answered, gazing up at her.

"Do you know who I am?" she asked, smiling.

"You're Aunt Em," I said as though she were asking me a silly question.

"Yes," she said. "This is who I really am."

"I know," I said, feeling my heart swell with love for her.

She smiled and faded from view. I went back to sleep.

When I awoke the next morning, her visit was the first thought on my mind. I turned to Ron and said, "Aunt Em died."

"How do you know?" Ron asked.

"Because she visited me."

Raising his eyebrows, he said smiling, "Did she say goodbye?"

"No," I said, "she didn't need to."

Joe called at nine to sadly announce that Aunt Em had died during the night.

I called Donna. "Uncle Raddy was right, after all," she remarked..

Now when I think of Aunt Em, I see her as the beautiful radiant being she really is. She and Uncle Raddy were important influences in my life, both while they lived and after they passed.

I think of them with love.

A TOUCH OF BLUE

2007

In 2004 Mom returned to Pittsburgh from Sarasota to finish out her life. I was retired, divorced for the second time and living alone. Mother and daughter, two single women, we decided to live together. In early March 2005, we moved into a townhouse near Pittsburgh, where I reside today. It has a master bedroom suite on the first floor and a large deck at the back.

My mother's warm personality and sense of humor kept her young even at age eighty-three. Veronica could tell a story and set a whole room to belly laughing. Her adoring family knew her to be a solid, loving person, a good listener, and one who could be trusted with secrets. Her dazzling white hair sparked brilliance into any color she wore, especially her signature shade of indigo blue.

Mom and I enjoyed shopping together, fixing up our home, and entertaining family and friends. Our most frequent visitor became Jim, the younger brother of my life-long friend, Linda. Jim, who was like family to us, had moved into our neighborhood after having lost his wife of thirty years to cancer. A few years earlier, he had also lost his mom, Mary, who had been like a second mother to me.

Jim comfortably adopted Veronica as his surrogate mom and a special bond grew between them. It wasn't long before the friendship Jim and I shared caught fire and we became more than just friends. He either joined us for dinner most evenings or took us out for dinner. The three of us became a family.

A one-time farmer, Jim loved to work outdoors with plants and trees. He used his skills to transform the wooded area beyond our deck into a garden paradise.

He planted holly, blue spruce, dogwood, and hemlock trees. Gathering large rocks from streams and roadsides, he also built a low wall of stone, a charming natural background for orange day lilies, yellow daffodils, hosta, ferns, vinca flowers, ivy, and fall blooming chrysanthemums.

In the midst of the colorful foliage on the ground, he placed a small rock waterfall, adding the balm of gently falling water. In the trees he hung bird feeders that attracted a gorgeous array—gold and purple finches, woodpeckers, cardinals, blue jays, mourning doves, grosbeaks, wrens, sparrows, and a few others.

From spring to fall, our spacious deck became an additional room where we gathered for meals, games, glasses of wine, and conversations. Separately Mom and I found peace and contentment there. I remember her sitting alone with a book in hand and glancing up to watch a hummingbird drink or a squirrel scurry across a deck railing.

One early November evening in 2005, as the three of us cleaned up after dinner, Mom, in the middle of an amusing story, suddenly started rambling nonsensically. Jim and I rushed to her. We gently lowered her to the floor and cushioned her head with a soft pillow. Recognizing that she was having a stroke, we called an ambulance and rushed her to the hospital.

I rode beside the ambulance driver while Jim followed in his car. Mom talked all the way to the hospital as though nothing at all was wrong. By the time we arrived, the left side of her face was sagging and her left arm and leg were paralyzed.

After the x-ray pictures and analyses were in, the emergency room doctor presented us with the option of injecting her with a clot-busting drug. He explained that it would be about forty minutes before the drug would take effect.

"It will either kill her or cure her," he warned. "I have no way of predicting what will happen."

We stood with the doctor as he explained the option and its risk to Mom. She thought for a minute then replied, "Give me the drug."

During the forty-minute wait, Jim and I sat at each side of Mom's bed talking softly and trying to appear as calm and confident as possible, even though we were inwardly anxious. I kept watching for adverse effects from the drug. None were evident.

A little more than forty minutes after the injection, the doctor and a few nurses gathered around Mom's bed.

"Veronica, can you raise your left arm for me?" he asked.

Her arm shot straight up! Everybody cheered!

"Can you raise your left leg?" He continued.

Her leg came straight up off the cot! We cheered loudly and applauded. I was surprised to see that more people had come into the area. Among them was my son, Stephen, who had just arrived from playing a gig in Pittsburgh.

Mom smiled broadly. Stephen, Jim, and I took turns hugging her and kissing her cheeks. The staff scurried off to complete paperwork and transport their star patient to a room.

Off to the side, one of the nurses explained that it was the first time they—including the doctor—had witnessed the drug working successfully. (I didn't ask if that meant the other patients had died.)

The following morning, my bespectacled mom was sitting up in bed reading her unfinished novel, which I had brought from home. I was in a chair nearby working a crossword puzzle.

After about ten days of observation and occupational therapy, Mom returned home from the hospital. Afterwards she followed a pattern of daily exercises until her motor skills seemed to stabilize. Sadly, during subsequent months, she regressed mentally.

Throughout 2006, her health gradually spiraled downward. Eventually we were unable to engage her in conversation or activities. Hoping she would find stimulation with persons her own age, we admitted her into assisted living at a nearby retirement home.

Her health continued its decline. She moved from assisted living into a nursing home, into a hospital room, and finally returned home with Hospice support.

On the morning of April 23, 2007, my dear Mom died peacefully at home. The previous night when I'd asked her if she wanted anything before I turned out the light, she answered softly, "I want out of here."

"Out of bed or out of this room?" I asked, testing to see if she meant what I thought she meant.

"Out of here." She lifted her feeble arm in a sweeping gesture, which I took to mean "out of this world."

"I understand, Mom," I said, kissing her on the forehead. "I'm here with you. I love you." She closed her eyes. I stood and studied her face. She looked peaceful, almost smiling.

I turned out the light and left the room. Later I returned and slept beside her hospital bed as I had done every night since her return from the hospital.

When I awoke the next morning Mom appeared to be asleep. I kissed her forehead and turned on the small stereo to play her favorites on a CD Jim had burned for her. The gorgeous music played softly while I showered and dressed—*The Lord's Prayer, Oh Danny Boy, Ave Maria, How Great Thou Art, He Walks with Me,* and several others.

Jim arrived and busied himself in the kitchen starting coffee, frying bacon, and making toast for us. Before I left our bedroom Mom was still asleep, breathing lightly. I greeted Jim and set the table.

Before we sat down to eat, I said, "I want to check on Mom again."

I returned to the bedroom and Jim followed.

Mom had stopped breathing. Her music played softly in the background as Jim and I stood with her in that sacred moment.

I took Mom's hand and whispered, "Go into the Light, Mom, be free." Kissing her forehead, I added, "I love you, Mom."

Jim kissed her hand and softly said his goodbye.

Dressed in an indigo blue suit, Mom's body was on view for only one day. The funeral service was held that same evening, attended by family and friends almost filling the large room. We dwelt on who Veronica was as a mother, relative, and friend, expressing our lasting impressions of her presence in our lives.

After the burial, grief hit me like a punch in the gut. Even though I knew she was in a better place, the stark absence of her was painful.

I filled my days with paperwork, housework, shopping, anything that kept me occupied. But I carried a constant ache within.

I found myself talking to Mom when I packed her clothes, did housework, cooked, or drove my car. The more I talked, the more I realized how much I had to say that had gone unsaid during our time together. Instead of alleviating my grief, my realization of things unsaid deepened it.

Several weeks later, I invited Jim to move in with me. He placed his house on the market and I threw myself into helping him prepare for potential buyers.

In the midst of those frenzied activities, I received news from Greensboro, North Carolina, that my close friend and Marion's godmother, Joyce, had died. Stricken with more sadness, I prepared to drive south the following morning. Jim was unable to go with me and wanted to book me a flight but I insisted on driving alone.

That evening I sat on the deck with my thoughts, realizing that my daily immersions into busy-ness had not eased my pain. My friend's death had intensified my grief. Then and there I decided to allow myself to feel the fullness of it, to be present with my agony rather than trying to suppress it.

Oh, I felt it all right! Burying my face in my hands, I yearned for release through tears. But I felt too mournful to cry.

Feeling like a boxer who'd been knocked to the mat, I slowly raised my head and stared out at our three-columned bird feeder. Perched on the bottom left rung was a bird I had never seen before. Its feathers were *indigo blue!*

My heart quickened! I felt Mom's presence. The bird just sat there without moving. It made no effort to eat. I *knew* that Mom was telling me through the indigo blue of the bird's feathers that she was near!

Jim stepped through the sliding door onto the deck.

Exhilarated, I said, "Jim, look at that bird!"

He looked at it curiously. "I wonder what it is," he said. "I've never seen one that color before."

"Right," I said. "It's indigo blue! What's that tell you?"

"What should it tell me?" he asked, confused. Jim, a retired computer engineer, was not open to spiritual or supernatural concepts. I knew this from our many conversations around the subject.

"It's from Mom! It's her color. She's letting me know she's here."

"Oh?" he asked. "Is that what you think?" I knew Jim didn't know what to say to me.

"It's what I *know*," I answered.

"I'll get the bird book and see if I can find it in there." He turned and went into the house.

I remained still, watching the gorgeous bird and feeling the warmth of Mom's presence. I sensed her voice and the sound of her laugh, which I had been trying to recall for weeks. My emotions surged and I cried, not knowing if my tears were from sadness or joy.

Returning with the opened book, Jim identified the bird as an indigo bunting. He read, "The smaller female is plain brown. Its diet is insects, tiny seeds, spiders and berries, and it nests in brushy pastures and in the edges of woodlands."

"So, there you have it," Jim concluded. "It's probably been around, but we just haven't seen it before." Seeing my tears he added, "Are you all right?"

"Maybe so, but that's not what I *feel*," I answered, swabbing tears and blowing my nose.

Tenderly placing his hand on my shoulder he said, "I understand how you feel, Em. It's your mom's favorite color." I could always count on Jim to be loving and sensitive. I felt that he was trying to mollify me in that emotional moment.

I shook my head. "No, Jim, it's not just the color, it's the *timing* of this bird's appearance. I *feel* Mom. She's touching in *now* when I need her the most!" I cried and laughed a little.

"Couldn't it be coincidental?" he asked gently. "The book says the indigo bunting lives in our area."

"Think about it, Jim. If you were Mom and wanted to give me a sign that you were near, wouldn't you do it in a way you knew I would understand? You would want to do it in a place where I would see it. The best place is here at a bird feeder." I gestured toward the feeder where the Indigo Bunting sat.

"Well…"

I interrupted. "And its color is like a name tag with 'Mom' written on it!" I said, watching the bird lovingly. "Not to mention the comfort it gives me."

"Well, I can't speak to that, sweetheart," he said, patting me on the shoulder. "I've no experience with such things." Jim bent down and kissed me lightly on the lips.

When I looked back, the bird was gone.

My drive to North Carolina went smoothly. Joyce's grown children and I sat up past midnight the first night catching up on our respective lives.

During the following day, we reminisced, cried, and laughed together.

Joyce had insisted on a memorial service and cremation rather than a traditional funeral. When the morning service ended the following day, I drove home.

Jim greeted me at the door and took me into his arms. I was glad to be back, but I felt drained. After we emptied the car and I freshened up, Jim led me out to the deck.

"I'll bring you a glass of wine and you can tell me about your trip."

"Did the Indigo Bunting return?" I asked.

"No, sweetheart," he answered, "I haven't seen it."

"I sure could use a visit from that special bird right now," I said, feeling emotionally drained and fatigued.

Jim went inside while I arranged chairs and placed a small table between them for our wine glasses. I sat in one of the chairs and looked out at the feeders.

Remarkably, there in the same location on the three-columned feeder sat the Indigo Bunting!

I was astonished and overjoyed! Mom's presence filled me once again!

Jim returned with two glasses of wine.

"Jim, look!" I said, pointing. "The Indigo Bunting's back!" My tears started to flow.

He stopped and looked. "Indeed it is," he said calmly. "How about that?"

"It's a signal from Mom again!" I exclaimed. "She knows I need her again right now. I *feel* her with me!" My tears continued but I felt comforted and lighthearted. I stood there smiling and feeling happy.

"I don't know, honey," Jim said kindly. "Buntings are supposedly common in this part of the country. You might be overreacting because we haven't seen them here before the other day."

I smiled knowing that Jim was lovingly trying to talk *sense* into me.

I dried my eyes. "It isn't just the bird's color and its perfect timing," I laughed and held out my arms, "it's also the comfort and happy feeling it brings me!"

Jim shrugged, "What can I tell you?"

"Should I consider all these coincidences?" I asked, smiling happily.

"I really can't answer that, sweetheart," Jim replied. "I just don't know."

Later, I called my daughter Cara in Michigan and reported my experiences with the Indigo Bunting. She and my other two children had always been very close to their grandmother.

"I wish something like that would happen to me," she said. "I think of Grandma all the time. I'd love to get a sign that she's around."

A month or so later, Jim and I were at a restaurant with

friends when my cell phone rang. Seeing that the call was from Cara, I excused myself and went outside to answer.

"Mom!" she was in tears. "I just got a message from Grandma! Now I know what you mean when you talk about *knowing!*"

"Tell me what happened," I said.

"Remember my telling you that our dear neighbor, Otto, died in February? Well, the house is empty now and I'm helping his daughter, Veronica, clean it up for the real-estate agent."

I was surprised to hear that the house had not already been sold but I didn't want to interrupt. I also thought about the coincidence that Otto's daughter had the same name as my mother.

"I was upstairs just now wiping down some shelving located in an alcove that opens out to a small balcony where Mike and I used to sit and have a glass of wine with Otto." Her voice was tremulous. "He always played his favorite song when we came here, 'Roses are Red, Violets are Blue' by Bobby Vinton—not only because it was his favorite," she let out a little laugh, "but also because he was impressed that I used to live near Bobby Vinton's home town of Canonsburg."

She continued, excited, "Anyway, as I reminisced about Otto, my mind turned to Grandma. I thought about how she died after Otto and, missing her as I do, I wondered why she hasn't given me an inkling of her presence."

"Honestly, Mom," she continued, "I've been looking for a blue bunting around our house, on our street, everywhere, but none's appeared. So as I'm here cleaning the shelves, it was as though all my thoughts converged through a kind of perfect storm: Otto, Bobby Vinton, Canonsburg, "Roses are Red, Violets are *Blue*," Otto's daughter named *Veronica*,

Grandma's color indigo *blue*, and the *Indigo Bunting* that came to your feeder. It suddenly hit me that the wallpaper around me is decorated with drawings of birds, but I'd never stopped to really look at it. Just as I was wondering if there might be a blue bunting there, I found myself staring at an Indigo Bunting! It is a lovely drawing with 'Indigo Bunting,' written in script next to it." She blew her nose.

"Oh, Mom, in that second, I *knew!* I almost laughed out loud! It was as if Grandma said, 'Hello, Cara. Here's an inkling for you: *I'm here.*'"

"Yes, Sweetheart," I laughed, "that's the way it happens." I felt exhilarated! "The timing is exact, and you *know* in that instant that you're connected. Tell me about the wallpaper."

"Yes...when I backed up, I saw that the wallpaper—which I hadn't really looked at before—is decorated with colorful birds of North America—birds like cardinals, yellow finches, robins, and so on. Their names are written beside them in elegant script. My eyes just *happened* to land on the Indigo Bunting," she exclaimed.

"I'm so happy that Grandma touched in with you, Cara!" I was filled with gratitude that she was able to experience and understand what I had tried to describe.

I said a mental *thank you* to Mom before adding, "Thanks for calling and sharing with me, Cara. You made my day!"

"Mine too," she answered. "I get it now. I understand what you mean when you say *knowing.*"

Months later, the family was gathered at our house to celebrate Labor Day. After dinner we gathered outside on the deck to enjoy the weather and the view. Cara looked out at the birds populating the feeders and asked Jim and me if we'd had any other sightings of the Indigo Bunting. We told her we had not.

Somebody asked what Cara meant. Most of the others

hadn't heard about our experiences, so Cara and I told our stories.

Afterwards, my son Stephen said, "Grandma and I were close. Why hasn't the bunting visited me?"

"I feel left out," my grandson added.

I had been standing with my back to the bird feeders. Cara, who stood facing me, shifted her gaze and her eyes popped wide open.

"Look!" She exclaimed, "There it is...the...the Indigo Bunting!"

Everybody moved forward to focus on the bird. Again, my heart quickened—and probably Cara's as well!

The Indigo Bunting sat on the bottom left rung of the three-columned feeder—the exact place it had appeared each time! It was as if Mom were saying to us, "I don't want to leave anybody out. I love all of you. Here's my inkling."

We stood in quiet awe of the bird's presence. I felt Mom's love. Joy welled up within me. I think everybody could *feel* Mom's presence. Desperate not to lose the moment, I ran inside and grabbed my camera in time to snap a few pictures.

Most surprised of all was Jim. Having dismissed all things supernatural, he couldn't explain the perfect *timing* of the Indigo Bunting's appearances. He had witnessed every one of them.

Glancing at him I asked, "Do you *still* think the Indigo Bunting's visits have been mere coincidences?"

"I think I'm starting to get it!" he announced, smiling and nodding his head.

We've never again seen the Indigo Bunting since that Labor Day in 2007.

We no longer have the need.

TODAY

LASTING EFFECTS

If you've never experienced the kinds of unexplainable happenings I've described, or even if you have, you might be struggling to understand—or even imagine—the possibility of such encounters.

Do you wonder if I've fabricated or embellished my narratives? Although I wouldn't blame you for thinking so, I can promise that I have not.

Each interlude was earthshaking to me. Anybody who was alive to experience Neil Armstrong's moon landing, the Kennedy Assassination, or the terrorist attack on the World Trade Center understands. One does not forget the details of earthshaking events. Excepting the reconstructed dialogue, the details of my spontaneous experiences are described exactly as they unfolded.

I have continually asked myself about my mystical interludes: *Why did they happen? What made them happen? What do they mean?* So far I haven't come up with answers to those questions. No matter. In the process of writing this book, I have come to realize that the most important question is this: *How have those experiences affected my life?*

For many years I lacked the perspective needed to sort out and discern their lasting influences. Now, with hindsight and maturity, I am able to distinguish and describe their effects.

The place to begin is when I "experienced God" to learn gratitude and forgiveness.

**Experiencing God in my childhood
shaped my outlook on life and also
enriched it beyond measure.**

My mother's hands-on way of teaching me about God's presence and power established for me that God exists. In addition, her daily example of praying from the heart rather than reciting memorized prayers taught me how to pray sincerely.

I began praying from my heart when I was five, often without receiving what I prayed for. For example, when I heard my parents arguing at night, I prayed for them to stop fighting and to love each other all the time. That didn't happen—certainly not the way my six-year-old mind thought it should!

At seven, I was devastated when Mom left Dad. Feeling abandoned by God, I could easily have stopped praying altogether. Fortunately, I did not. Desperate for hope, I clung to my mother's words, "God works in His own time...you'll get an answer...be patient, sweetheart."

When Mom returned to us after nine months, I felt overwhelming *gratitude!* Feeling deep gratitude at an early age was a precious gift. Most important to me at the time was my *knowing* that God had heard my prayers and answered them. I believe that to this day. The evidence can be seen in the way our lives unfolded throughout the following years.

After Mom came back and we became a family again Dad no longer got drunk with his buddies after work. He stayed home with us in the evenings and we grew and thrived as a family. Such transformation in a person doesn't happen overnight. Maybe Mom was gone for as long as was needed for Dad to change his ways. God works in his own time.

My parents remained together in marriage for the rest of their lives while providing a stable, loving home for my brothers and me. Their lifelong love was a gift to us and to their grandchildren, profound and beneficial beyond calculation.

Observing our parents transform and grow through their separation and reunion modeled important life lessons for us.

For one thing, we saw that change and renewal can happen through passionate effort. We also witnessed the ways in which our parents were mutually empowered through their renewed relationship. They encouraged and supported each other to learn new skills and accomplish goals. We saw our mom develop into an excellent cook, seamstress and artist. In her later years she sold many of her paintings. We watched our dad, who dropped out of school after the eighth grade, continue his education in coal mining to become a regional manager of western Pennsylvania coal mines for the Jones and Laughlin Steel Corporation. During my early years these were my heart's first lessons in "love conquers all."

Learning to forgive at the tender age of eight, with the help of Pastor McCready, was nothing short of a miracle. Had I not trusted God's instruction to forgive, I might have grown up hating, blaming, and resenting Aunt Em. I might have even transferred those feelings to others as I encountered failures and woes, common to all lives. My outlook on the world would likely have been rooted in suspicion, fear, and anger.

Instead, this understanding has enabled me to take responsibility for my own mistakes. I have been able to persevere through life's challenges without blaming others for my distress. Those prayer experiences also forged my lifelong faith in a loving ever-present Supreme Being.

**My mystical interludes revealed
that love is my reason for being.**

When I was a child, I learned some things about the power of love. God's love for me and also Pastor McCready's love for me fueled my efforts to forgive. Once I started to forgive Aunt Em, my love for her began to grow. I learned an important life lesson: love enables forgiveness: forgiveness enables love.

The most profound and significant experience of love came later when I stood in the presence of Divine Love during my near-death experience (NDE). To those who have not had such a life-changing event, there is no way to describe its power. Its effect on my life has been so significant, I find it impossible to summarize. I'll just highlight some of the fundamentals.

In the immediate aftermath of the NDE, I was able to comprehend the kind of love that might have inspired people like Mother Theresa and Albert Schweitzer to dedicate their lives to serving the needs of others, regardless of risks to themselves. Within my own heart, love and compassion for people of every race, religion, sexual preference, or physical difference arose and flourished throughout my life. Words and deeds based on racism or loveless discrimination trouble me deeply to this day. My view of the human race is that we, meaning *all* of us, are brothers and sisters created by, and intrinsic to the Universal Loving Spirit, our Creator—That or Who is named and worshipped in every language on earth.

Marion and the orange glasses, and Mom and the Indigo

Bunting, conveyed to me that love shared on earth does not end at death. Just as we don't stop loving people after they die, those who love us at their transitions can continue to express their love to us if we are awake to that possibility.

Seeing myself in a past life and believing that I will return to this physical plane in another body begs the question *Why?* Why might I come back as another personality? I surmise it would be for the most important reason to exist: love.

Love operates in a myriad of mysterious ways. I doubt that it can ever be fully known or understood. Love is the universal nurturer of life. We know that when love is absent, human life diminishes and distorts. My instinct is that the purpose of rebirth is for learning and experiencing love—or its absence—so that love can be known in all its bearings.

The near-death experience eliminated my fear of death.

My youthful fear of death and dying began with my dear friend Mrs. Morrow, a kind neighbor who lived on our street about four houses away. Mrs. Morrow, a soft and round elderly woman with white hair and glasses, spent most of the temperate days from spring to fall sitting in her cushioned wicker chair on her shaded front porch. A widow with time on her hands, she enjoyed engaging in light conversation with sidewalk folks passing by on their way to the grocery store, post office or any other place in our small town.

We became acquainted as I was ending the third grade and running errands that took me past her house almost every day. Our frequent chats kindled invitations to return for cookies and milk after my errands were finished for the day. In a short time, visiting Mrs. Morrow became one of my favorite things to do.

It wasn't just the scrumptious homemade cookies that drew me to her. It was her loving kindness, and her rapt attention to my every word. Whenever I told her about an upcoming test or book I was reading, she later remembered the smallest details and asked intriguing follow-up questions that inspired my own learning and self-reflection.

By the end of summer, Mrs. Morrow started braiding my hair into short pigtails. She even bought me ribbons and barrettes. I grew to love her the way I loved my grandmothers.

I entered the fourth grade and autumn began. After the weather turned chilly I met with Mrs. Morrow less and less. One cold and dreary Saturday I decided to pay her a visit. I knocked on the front door and stood admiring the beautiful wreath of flowers that adorned it. Mrs. Morrow's daughter, whom I had met once before, opened the door.

Reaching out warmly, she said, "Oh, you've come to see Mother! Come in, come in." She pulled me inside.

Before I could ask a question, she ushered me around the corner into the large living room and up to a coffin holding Mrs. Morrow's corpse!

Until that moment I had never seen a dead person or a real coffin. I stood dumbfounded and speechless. My facial expression must have conveyed utter shock. Mrs. Morrow, my dear, grandmotherly friend was not Mrs. Morrow anymore! She was now a frightening, alien dead person!

"Oh, Emily. You didn't know Mom passed, did you?"

I shook my head, unable to speak and finding it hard to breathe.

"Oh, I'm so sorry. I thought for sure you knew." She stood compassionately beside me.

As I stared at Mrs. Morrow's white, lifeless face, I thought I saw her eyes open. Then I thought I saw her lips move. My heart raced.

"I know it's hard to believe," the daughter said. "She's been such a big part of our lives."

After a silent pause she whispered, "I've always been told that touching the body has a way of convincing us that the person is no longer with us."

Petrified at the thought, I didn't move.

"You might want to try it. It might help the way you're feeling."

I looked at the pleated cloth lining the open lid of the coffin and imagined somebody closing the lid. It would be dark and suffocating inside. Then the casket would be locked and lowered into the earth. My every breath seemed to catch in my chest.

"Here, why don't you give it a try?" She raised my limp hand and gently placed it on top of a cold, hard, extraterrestrial-like hand inside the coffin. I flinched and jerked away thinking I might throw up.

Leading me away from the casket Mrs. Morrow's daughter said, "Come into the kitchen for some hot chocolate, why don't you?"

"No, thank you. I have to go home." I turned the corner and rushed out the door.

For years afterward, nightmares roiled my sleep. Like in so many horror films, dead people came back to life and grabbed me, trying to pull me into their graves. Speaking of horror films, *Frankenstein and Dracula* were favorites at our town's little movie theater. Even though my parents wouldn't allow us to see those films, Boris and Bela—two iconic actors famous for playing dead people who weren't *really* dead—would pop up in previews to terrify me!

The very thought of being buried terrified me— buried alive especially. Everything associated with death frightened me. Even walking past a funeral home gave me a creepy feeling. People around me didn't seem to give much thought to death or care to talk about it. My horror of death, corpses and caskets caused me to feel set apart from others as I grew.

When I became a teenager, I wanted to acquire a more "normal" attitude by reading about religions other than Christianity. Meanwhile I attended church, questioned the minister and delved into Bible narratives about death. I found little to assuage my fear.

The Bible said Christ was dead for three days before he came back to life. In my fearful mind, that meant He was trapped in that cold dark tomb for three days! Is that what we should expect? Christ raised Lazarus from the dead. That caused me to wonder if some tiny nerve within us might keep ticking imperceptibly even after we're buried while we waited for heaven, hell, or rebirth. The story of the Rapture predicting that Christ's return to earth will summon all believers up from their graves only terrified me more.

The paralyzing fear ended with my near-death experience in 1956. Afterwards I understood death to be a natural, joyful process of the soul rejoining its Loving Source. As I watched bodies step off the train, the revelation to me was that each body dissolved as its soul became One with the eternal, loving Light.

I came to perceive the true "me" as my eternal soul, not my body. In this life my soul is playing out the human character of "Emily" with all her flaws, foibles, failures and successes. "Emily" is only a facet of who I *really* am.

Both the past-life vision and
near-death experience inspired
my spiritual beliefs.

The concept of reincarnation came to me when I was a child, even before I knew it had a name. As I grew and studied various religions, I discovered that the belief predated Christianity in several Asian religions and was also held by early Christians. My visit to myself as a girl in Siam crystallized my belief in the eternal cycle of birth, return to Oneness in the eternal universe of a Loving Spirit, and rebirth in human form on earth.

My childhood idea of God sitting on a throne in heaven was replaced by my understanding of God as Infinite Loving Intelligent Consciousness, omnipotent and omnipresent throughout our universe and beyond, dwelling also within each of us as Soul. Again, I find myself entangled in words too inadequate to describe transcendent concepts.

I feel quite foolish attempting to name or describe That which we call God. My consolation is that I am not alone in this quandary. Our Creator has been given at least 114 different descriptions throughout the world. According to my quick search, Christianity describes God as good, gracious, holy, incomprehensible, infinite, jealous, loving, mysterious, omniscient, omnipresent, righteous, true, transcendent, forgiving, wrathful, and the list goes on.

During my NDE I saw nobody standing at the entrance checking credentials to determine if souls were Christian, Jewish, Muslim, Buddhist, or of any other religion. Nobody was sitting in judgment to banish them to hell. The people I saw became One with the Light. From what I have experienced, I strongly believe that our Creator's Love transcends all the religious, racial, sexual, cultural, and political barriers we, ourselves, have raised to separate and divide humans from humans.

Until my NDE, I hadn't given much thought to whether angels existed. Yet the angel I saw was magnificent. It appeared to me as male. In my mind, maleness implies inherent strength. The wings that carried him to the ground conveyed movement and mobility. The Bible defines angels as messengers from God. I have derived from both these sources that angels can swiftly and powerfully attend to certain emergencies in our lives to lift us out of danger and also change certain outcomes. There have been more than a few occasions when I felt that my guardian angel came to my rescue.

I recall a wintry evening when I paused before leaving home to attach an angel pin to my sweater. The pin, which I was wearing for the first time, had been a gift from a student.

Later that evening when I started my drive home, the roads had turned icy and dangerous. Entering Interstate 70 West from an entrance ramp, my car's tires spun on the ice, then suddenly gained traction. The car shot car onto the highway just as a speeding eighteen-wheeler whizzed by, striking the car on the driver's side, and smashing it into a guardrail. Fortunately I was strapped inside my seat belt or I would have been violently thrown by the impact which left the vehicle badly damaged.

The windshield had a large hole in it and several windows were blown out, including the one in the driver's door. Broken glass covered everything inside. I was severely shaken, but ultimately, I didn't have so much as a scratch from the collision. Nobody, including the police, the ambulance medics and the truck driver could believe I was uninjured.

Later that night I noticed the angel pin on my sweater. I had a big *ah-ha*. Later I confessed to my husband and my cousin Dorothy that I believed my angel had saved me from harm. I still do.

The mystical interludes
expanded my awareness.

Jim and I joke about the different ways we perceive things and make decisions. He's analytical; I'm spontaneous. He makes plans and follows the book; I follow my intuition.

When we need groceries I scribble a list then quickly head to the store. Jim doesn't budge until he checks the time (to avoid rush-hour traffic), checks road closings and also checks the weather.

Both our methods work—one is not better or worse than the other. Through observing my intuitive reactions Jim concedes that I have an awareness that he doesn't have. For example the moment I saw the Indigo Bunting perched on our bird feeder, my heart resonated to its presence. I was *aware* that Mom was signaling, "I'm still with you." When I pointed out the bird to Jim, his awareness was limited to only one aspect: the indigo blue bird was a newcomer to our woods. He reacted with curiosity by fetching his book and researching its identity.

He didn't realize what he had missed until much later.

"At first, linking that indigo color to Veronica didn't occur to me," he said, "but after being present during each of the bunting's perfectly timed visits, and also learning of Cara's experience, it struck me; those were not coincidences!" He smiled, then added, "I'm starting to get it."

Expanded awareness is a gift that has evolved in me— and can evolve in us all, if we allow it. I have learned to trust it. There are countless ways expanded awareness has manifested in my life. One of the most significant of these happened after I'd retired from teaching.

During my early morning walk through the small cemetery near my house, I was startled out of my wits by a large crow. From out of nowhere, it streaked past my face loudly screaming an urgent "CAW, CAW!" As my heart settled back into its normal beat, I became *aware* that my deceased brother Steve was alerting me to an upcoming crisis. I *felt* it, even though I had never before associated Steve with a crow.

Dreading what the crisis might be, I ended my walk and hurried home.

Once there I finished all the laundry, prepared soup and chili for freezing, and caught up on housework. I was preparing to be away from home or occupied for several days with no idea if I might be leaving or what I was preparing for.

During dinner that evening, I told my husband Ron I had a feeling some crisis was coming up that might take me away from home.

"We'll see, won't we," he said, sympathetically. "If something comes up, you'll do what you need to do. I'll be fine here." I was grateful for his support and understanding.

The day passed normally until nearly eleven o'clock that night. The house phone rang. It was Luanne, my close friend from New Hampshire. She was calling from her car while following behind an ambulance carrying her husband Sam to the hospital. Lu had no family other than her invalid mother living in Pittsburgh. Her young daughter Amy was away at school.

"Can you come?" Lu asked, her voice shaking from having described what was happening.

"I'll get there as soon as I can," I replied.

Sam, age fifty-five, had been recovering from lung surgery. He and my brother Steve had been best friends. Sam stood with our family at Steve's bedside when he died. He and Lu were like brother and sister to me.

I booked an emergency flight which got me to the hospital at around four a.m. to find Lu waiting outside the intensive care unit. She asked the nurse to admit me into Sam's room.

Hooked up to IVs and oxygen, he was sitting up in bed able to talk with me. Lu and I took turns visiting his room, leaving intervals for him to rest. Each of us was able to get him to smile sometimes. As we shared those incidents, we drew hope from them.

After two tense and weary days, Sam's doctor requested a meeting with Luanne. Much to her shock and grief, the doctor informed her that Sam's life was soon coming to an end. He asked her permission to arrange Sam's transfer to a hospice facility.

Sam died there two days later.

I was there to help Lu in any way I could, from preparing a memorial service near their home to arranging transport of Sam's body back to Pittsburgh for burial in his family's chosen cemetery. A few days later Luanne, her daughter Amy and I returned to Pittsburgh on the same plane that carried Sam's body. His burial took place two and a half days afterward.

Some time after Luanne and Amy returned to New Hampshire, I resumed my normal activities as best I could. They included my usual early morning walk in the small cemetery. The routine was to walk two loops on the asphalt road that outlined the cemetery's perimeter. As I ascended the hill on the first loop I thought about the crow's loud caws a few weeks earlier and my intuitive *knowing* that it was a warning from my brother.

In my mind, I spoke to Steve saying, *Was that you?*
Nothing.

Come on, Steve, I know you were giving me a heads up. Please give me an answer!

Nothing.

I rounded the bottom of the cemetery and started the second loop up the hill. There, lying perfectly centered on the path before me, was a crow's feather! I *knew* my question had been answered. I laughed and picked up the feather, feeling Steve's closeness along with his sense of humor.

That feather will always remain with me. It is pinned to my bedroom wall as I write these words.

Without an expanded awareness I would have missed the "heads up" and also the intimate connection with my late brother.

The interludes made me unafraid of most things and prone to taking risks.

Thinking back on my earlier fear of death and some of the fears I've held in the past, I've concluded that most were unfounded and sometimes obstructive. I'm not talking about fear that comes from an imminent threat like a charging wild animal or mugger with a weapon. I'm talking about self-generated fears, such as fear of the future, fear of speaking out in a group, or fear of failure.

Until now, I have not attempted to write a book, let alone a book exposing my personal life and some of my most intimate experiences. It's taken me a long time to get here. Publicizing this work reminds me of a nightmare I used to have of being shoved naked onto a stage before a huge audience. It's frightening. But here I am.

I undertook a different sort of risk on a recent birthday by parachuting from an airplane for the first time. Why did I do it? Because it was on my bucket list. When I am on my deathbed, I will not rue my failure to take the plunge. Rather, I'll relive my joyful exhilaration from the thrill of pushing off into sky and racing gloriously through white wispy clouds, then gliding onto the emerald green landing strip right on target!

They have inspired me to be happy and grateful.

Although I've struggled with problems and suffered painful losses and heartaches like everybody else, I've lived, and continue to live a happy life. My struggles, griefs and sorrows have not diminished my joy, hope and faith. All my experiences have taught that I am never alone and never without guidance or hope. Beginning each day with gratitude gives me a bright outlook. Holding love in my heart for all humanity and also feeling loved get me through life's disappointments and tragedies.

Today I realize that my mystical experiences were precious gifts. It's my regret that for so many years I questioned why and how those events were happening, rather than recognizing that they were expanding my awareness and also deepening my understanding of love and life.

TOMORROW

A NEW HORIZON

The subtitle of this book is "An Ordinary Person's Extraordinary Experiences." I hope you agree that I have not exaggerated. I am clearly an ordinary, flawed person whose experiences have been extraordinary.

What I've presented in this book are those unexplainable events and what I have derived from them as I continue to keep an open mind. Although my intention is to encourage and inspire, nothing I have described is meant to teach, persuade, or promote a particular point of view or belief.

I regret that I didn't do more to seek out others like myself during past years when I felt "different" from my friends because of my mystical episodes. When the near-death experience happened, I had never heard of such a thing. There was no easy way to talk about it, let alone attempt to describe it. However, times have changed. Today, when I enter the letters NDE into a search engine, the screen fills with personal accounts and names of research organizations! This adds to my belief that there are many, many people who share experiences similar to mine.

It is my deep hope that other ordinary people who have experienced mystical events will come forward. Talk about them, write about them, blog about them if you are so inspired—but most of all, grow through them!

I am still a seeker, ever evolving. Perhaps you are, too. If any element of what I have described has inspired you to share your mystical interludes, I have done what I intended to do.

My latest question is this: What common elements might we discover among the extraordinary experiences of all who come forward and share them?

Perhaps we'll find out together.*

I look forward to a new horizon in human awareness.

*See *A Personal Invitation* on page 184.

ABOUT THE AUTHOR

Emily Rodavich is a product of several small industrial communities in the Pittsburgh area. She attended Indiana University of Pennsylvania and later graduated from Waynesburg University in Waynesburg, Pennsylvania.

Mystical Interludes is her first book, though her artistic endeavors have bloomed elsewhere.

In 1968 she collaborated with Jay Christopher in writing lyrics for a musical written by Christopher and her pianist husband, Carl Geruschat. The musical, *Your Most Humble Servant,* based on the lives of Samuel Johnson and his biographer James Boswell, was produced at the White Barn Theater in Irwin, Pennsylvania, and also in a small theater in London, England.

While teaching high school English, she directed school plays and also patented a hands-on methodology for teaching the parts of speech.

Emily has traveled to various parts of the United States and to Europe, Egypt, China, Thailand, and Israel partly to explore spiritual, religious, and supernatural mysteries, including her own.

She is mother to three children and grandmother to two grandsons and two granddaughters. Her offspring include several talented musicians and singer/songwriters.

Visit www.emilyrodavich.com.

A PERSONAL INVITATION

Have you ever had a mystical interlude of your own? Many people I've talked with have reported experiencing one or two mystical incidents, yet not enough to fill a book. If you are one of those people, consider submitting a description of your experience for potential publication in the forthcoming book, *Mystical Interludes II: A Collection of Ordinary People's Mystical Experiences.* For information, visit www.mysticalinterludes.com.

Finally if you are inclined to leave a review where you purchased *Mystical Interludes* and/or on any other social media websites where you participate, your invaluable feedback will help us shape the next edition.

Made in the USA
Middletown, DE
14 May 2020

94700798R00111